Praise for
Slices: Observations from the Wrong Side of the Fairway

"*Slices* will make you forget all about those flubbed chips and missed putts, because you'll be too busy laughing."
  ~ *John Tenpenny, Editor*, Fairways

"I.J. Schecter may someday break 100, but let's hope not—it's far too much fun cheering him along in the attempt."
  ~ *Jason Sowards, Editor*, Golf Illustrated

"I.J. Schecter reminds us that the most important skill in golf isn't driving, chipping or putting, but the ability to laugh."
  ~ *Neil Yack, Director of Instruction, Richmond Hill Golf Club*

"Take this trip with I.J. Schecter as he tries to convince himself, and you, that he's found the secret (or is that secrets?) to a better swing. Laugh along while he dreams of greater glories on the course or goes up against famous players during a fantastical round of mini-golf. Get to know his Uncle Hugh—you probably have an Uncle Hugh in your golfing life. Sit back and take it all in as Schecter conveys you on a happy-go-lucky ride through the wonderful and wondrous world of golf."
  ~ *Lorne Rubenstein*

Slices

To Sam,

May your drives fly straight,
your approaches stick and your
putts find the back of the cup!

Best,

observations from the
wrong side of the fairway

I.J. Schecter

WILEY

John Wiley & Sons Canada, Ltd.

National Library of Canada Cataloguing in Publication Data

Schecter, I. J., 1971-
    Slices : observations from the wrong side of the fairway / I.J. Schecter.

Includes index.
ISBN 13 978-0-470-83734-4
ISBN 10 0-470-83734-9

1. Golf—Humor. I. Title.

GV967.S33 2006   796.352'02'07   C2005-907751-4

Production Credits:
Cover design: Ian Koo
Front cover image: Royalty-Free/Getty Images
Interior text design: Adrian So

Printer: Printcrafters

John Wiley & Sons Canada, Ltd.
6045 Freemont Blvd.
Mississauga, Ontario
L5R 4J3

Printed in Canada
1 2 3 4 5 PC 10 09 08 07 06

"Home on the Range" originally appeared in the August 2004 issue of *Golf Monthly* as "At home on the range"

"Young Drivers" originally appeared in the December 2004 issue of *Golf Monthly* as "I suck—big time!"

"A Christmas Miracle" originally appeared in the January 2005 issue of *Golf Monthly* as "Winter wonderland"

"With Resolve" originally appeared in the February 2005 issue of *Golf Monthly* as "Desperate Measures"

"Ten Reasons I'll (Probably) Never Take a Golf Lesson" originally appeared in the October 2002 issue of *Golf Journal* as "10 Reasons I'll Never Take a Golf Lesson"

"Uncle Hugh's Rules for Maintaining a Ten Handicap" originally appeared in the July 2004 issue of *Golf Monthly*

"Next on the Tee, Shaq" originally appeared in the July 2003 issue of *Golf Monthly* as "Next on the tee—George W Bush"

"Longest Drive? How About Biggest Slice?" originally appeared in the March 2003 issue of *Golf Monthly* as "The game is up"

"Easy Ryder" originally appeared in the October 2004 issue of *Golf Monthly* as "A fair contest"

"The Duffer's Guide to Poise, Panache and Popularity" originally appeared in the December 2003 issue of *Golf Monthly* as "The high-handicapper's guide to panache and popularity"

"Lob Wedge or Hand Shears?" originally appeared in the March 2005 issue of *Golf Monthly* as "Five-iron or hand shears?"

"Putting My Game to the Test" originally appeared in the September 2004 issue of *Golf Monthly* as "Who's to blame?"

"Everything I Needed to Know About Golf I Learned from My Toddler" originally appeared in the August 2005 issue of *GOLF Canada* as "Child's play"

For Stephanie

Contents

Acknowledgments

Without the contributions of a number of people, this book would amount to little more than endless descriptions of my dreadful golf game. Come to think of it, it may still amount to little more than that, but lots of people were nonetheless instrumental in helping me write it.

Brent Rogers, at Eagles Nest in Toronto, and Mark Reid, at The Breakers in West Palm Beach, forever changed the way I look at a golf course by showing me what goes on before the sun comes up and after it goes down. Michael Webster, at the Men's Salon Hairstyling and Barbershop in Toronto's sparkling BCE Place, not only helped even out my sideburns but also delighted me with stories of his ongoing golf exploits. My friend Ira Smith happily accepted my badgering to provide details of his magical round at Copper Creek Golf Club in Toronto. Several members of South Florida's Palm Beach golf community, including Tim O'Connor at the Breakers Ocean Course, Joe Demino at Boca Raton Resort &

Club, John Gardner at PGA National Golf and Sports Club, Brian Marchi at Emerald Dunes Golf Course and the good folks at Delray Beach Golf Club, allowed me onto their courses even after I'd alerted them to the horrors they might witness. Kevin Pauley at Royal Niagara Golf Club was kind enough to host my playing partners and me on a splendid afternoon that would have been memorable for the clubhouse burgers alone.

Others deserve special acknowledgement. I'd like to thank my wife's young cousins Daniel and Jeremy Goldlist for showing me how the new generation plays the game, and their father, Barry, for playing it the way I do.

I'm indebted to Dow Finsterwald Sr., winner of the 1958 PGA Championship and one of golf's top players for over a decade, for taking me on a mental walk through the final holes of a major, the closest I'll ever get to actually winning one. By acting like just another golf enthusiast, as opposed to a guy who regularly faced off with Palmer and Snead, Dow showed me what a true champion is.

I'm deeply grateful to Scott Myles of Don Valley Golf Course in Toronto. Scott is a charismatic instructor and relentless optimist who somehow turned my swing into something that can occasionally persuade a golf ball to fly in the general direction of its target. That puts him in the same category as David Copperfield.

I treasure every moment I've shared with my fellow members of the formidable RAID Tour—Rob Sheinfeld, David Bleiwas and Andrew Weir. If you want to remember their names, best to do it now, since you'll never hear about them for their golf games. In particular I'd like to thank Andrew, with whom I've been friends longer than with anyone else in the world, for improving several of these essays by placing them under his ruthless but benevolent editing knife.

My profound thanks goes to Jane Carter and the entire team at *Golf Monthly*, the magazine in which a number of these pieces originally appeared, as well as to John Tenpenny, formerly of *GOLF Canada*, and Cathrine Wolf, of the former *Golf Journal*, who made space for my ramblings about this marvelous, infuriating sport.

I can't express appreciation enough to my editor at Wiley, Karen Milner. Not only is Karen an astute reader, but she's also a certifiable sports nut. When, during one of our early meetings, she slid across the table a copy of the twentieth anniversary edition of Ken Dryden's *The Game* with no idea that the original version had changed my life when I'd read it as a twelve-year-old, I knew I'd found a kindred spirit.

Thank you to my three-year-old son, Julian, for periodically hijacking my laptop and helping me get through mental blocks by composing sentences like EBEBmeka;BiMIEbia;y888, and my one-year-old, Oliver, for his equal flair at loosening my thinking, usually by banging a plastic golf club against the floor and saying things like, "Aaahhhhhhhhhhhh!"

Finally, when one comes to express his gratitude to the person who stands by his side every day, words inevitably fall short. My wife, Stephanie, is my source of strength, my editor-in-residence and my inspiration to always do better. I only hope she knows how much I love her for her warmth, support, patience and insight, but mostly for being extremely pretty.

Preface

During one summer a few years ago, I managed to get out on the course only twice in the first six weeks of the season. The first time out, I shot 92—for me, a magical round. I still have no idea how I did it. In a way, I don't even remember the round. I was in some kind of zone. It's a shame I've never been back.

The next round, I shot 121. I'm not kidding. That's a 29 stroke difference. I couldn't hit a single shot. I might as well have been wearing oven mitts. It was horrific (to me, at least; to my playing partners, it was a hoot).

These two rounds represent everything I love about golf. Those who play it impressively keep in mind that the ups need to be taken with a grain of salt and the downs will eventually pass (unless you're shooting 121, in which case it's pretty much downs all the way). I love the polarity, and intensity, of golf's two primary emotions: on one hand, after you hit a good shot, the feeling that you're a golfer of towering skill, impeccable instincts and perfect grace, and on the other, after you hit a bad shot, the belief that, when you were born, God got to thinking about what would be the most amusing thing to deny you in life and eventually went with motor skills.

I love the anticipation I feel before every round, the genuine belief that I will do better today. I don't know whether this is because I simply can't bear the thought of doing worse, but I think every other golfer feels it, too. Most touring professionals would laugh themselves silly to hear that a magical round resulted in a score of 92. After all, their good rounds are *30* strokes better. But the point is that, whether it's a 62 being stalked by a top PGA player or a 92 being hunted by a weekend duffer, golf represents the lifelong pursuit of tiny improvements—and that's a good lesson for anybody.

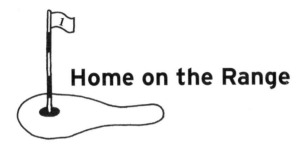

Home on the Range

If golf has taught me anything—besides how to string together expletives in ways that would make Eminem blush—it's that you can trust the magic that occurs on the practice range as much as you can trust a piranha that has skipped a feed. The range contains a bizarre magnetic field that causes every ball to fly as straight and true as if it were a bead on a string. This same benign presence somehow vanishes on every first tee, replaced by random electrical impulses that send your ball on trajectories you never imagined—except in nightmares—as though some warped overlord were amusing himself by flicking the magnetization on and off. This would make sense, in fact. After all, if God has a sense of humor, wouldn't a golf course be the ideal place to abuse it?

The range is an alternate universe, a glorious sub-reality in which slices, shanks and blocks are wiped from the realm of possibility and we all become Tiger Woods, or at least Phil Mickelson. On the range, pulses are relaxed, blood pressure is low and anxiety is non-existent. On the range, one's greatest pressure concerns whether his sunblock has an adequate SPF.

Today, I vow not to fall for it. I've had enough false epiphanies over the years—those *A-HA!* moments when I inadvertently fix the one thing that's been hindering my game all this time—to know when I'm being fooled.

So this morning, sharing a pail of balls with my friend Dave— the two others in our usual four, Rob and Andrew, sharing a pail as well—I choose instead to savor the warm air, the blue sky, the scent of freshly cut grass. Relishing the easy banter passing between us, I flip my 8-iron out of the bag and roll a striped black ball onto the practice mat.

After a handful of shots, an interesting thing happens. As I strike the ball and watch it fly in the actual direction I intended, a sense of something, a certain awareness, rises in me. I changed something just now. My elbow, yes—I kept my back elbow in a fraction of a second longer. An accident, maybe, but an intriguing one.

Then again, maybe it was no accident. Perhaps my instincts just knew to make this adjustment. This is a curious thought, since any adjustment I've ever made on a golf course has actually served to worsen my game.

I roll another ball onto the mat and, amazingly, create the same result. Two good shots in a row. I'm as scared and exhilarated as a scientist who realizes his new discovery could just as easily save the world or destroy it.

Keeping my back elbow tucked in works for the 7-iron, too, and the 6, and then, miracle of miracles, the lob wedge. It works with the 3-iron and the 4. Dave, noticing my intense focus—and possibly alarmed by the extent to which I'm murmuring to myself—directs his conversation toward Rob and Andrew.

I pull out the driver, knowing this breakthrough will never transfer to my woods. But it does. Half a dozen lovely practice drives later, I don't know what to believe, other than the certainty that, at long last, I've found the secret, the magical tweak that has eluded me all these years. It was so simple! How could I not have figured this out sooner?

We finish our pails and head for the first tee. I can barely contain a mad grin as visions of low 90s and high 80s dance in my head. I feel almost sorry for the others; no matter how well they play today, they have no idea what's about to hit them. The tiny adjustment is sure to lower my score by ... I become giddy just thinking about it. Five strokes? *Ten?*

Standing in a diamond configuration, we twirl a tee in the air to see who hits first. It lands pointing slightly closer to me than to Andrew. Normally, this would get my nerves hopping. Standard first-tee butterflies are bad enough; when I have to hit first, they become pterodactyls. But not today.

I address the ball. The ball doesn't appear concerned. Over my shoulder I hear the usual predictions.

"Left, into the woods."

"Pop up."

"Off the heel. Just past the ladies' tees."

As I issue my brain the reminder—what was it ... something about my elbow?—my muscles seem to stiffen as one, as though succumbing to rigor mortis while I'm still alive. I step back and perform a few extra neck stretches. "Not comfortable yet, boys."

"Who's ever comfortable?" says Rob.

I step back up and, without over-thinking it, decide simply to rip at the ball. Unfortunately, I forget that not over-thinking is the same as not thinking. My dismal pop-up—satisfying Dave's prediction, the bastard—doesn't quite make the front edge of the fairway. This feels something like approaching a girl you'd like to seduce and tripping on your shoelace instead. I remind myself to remind myself about the back elbow on the next shot.

But a moment before that next shot—a 3-wood; damn my desire to use a 3-wood against all good sense—Andrew asks how my sister, six months pregnant, is feeling. I tell him she's feeling good and then proceed to send my ball slicing into the woods as though it saw something terrifying in mid-flight. Cursing Andrew for caring about my sister, I remind myself to take a moment before the *next* shot to remember the riddle I solved on the range.

Before that shot, Dave asks us whether we think he needs new golf shoes. I skull my 9-iron, accidentally getting the ball near the green anyway. When we're all finally on, and I stand over my putt, Rob remembers to tell us he ran into a high school flame of mine a few days earlier. With my ball now resembling a genetically blessed seventeen-year-old girl, I might as well record a four-putt.

The others aren't throwing me off my game intentionally. These exchanges simply represent the recreational golfer's paradox: Though any given round is enjoyed mostly for its camaraderie, one requires absolute concentration just to avoid a disastrous score. In other words, what separates the professional golfer from the weekend duffer? The pro is actually thinking about golf most of the time he's playing it.

At the fifth, a par 3 over a lake that seems to swell every time I glance upward, I finally remember to concentrate on my back elbow. Unfortunately, the other 29 parts of my swing give way in unison, providing the lake another morsel in an endless meal. Taking an extra club, I grab a new ball from my bag, get set again … and whistle this one over the green.

Hell with the back elbow, I decide. This time, just swing away and go for broke. What was I doing thinking I'd found the secret? Time for analysis to take a back seat and natural athleticism and coordination to shine through.

Athleticism and coordination, recognizing there's little they can contribute to golf, decide not to participate. By the time we reach the turn, my earlier vision of a score in the 90s is replaced by a new one: me impaling myself on a sand wedge.

So goes the rest of the round. My back elbow, for all the good it's doing, might as well be a spaghetti noodle. Instead, I try to remember past adjustments that seemed worthwhile: keeping my head down; keeping the club face square; not opening my hips too early; not opening my hips too late; not thinking of a foot-long meatball sub at the top of my backswing.

The other three are having their own problems, making my round somewhat more tolerable. Dave is carving up the fairways like an archaeologist, one moment ripping a clean 5-wood 180 yards toward the green, the next lofting a chunk of earth the size of my shoe 20 feet ahead. Rob, reading the course like it's written in a foreign language, keeps hitting short or long on his approaches as though he's aiming for a different flag than the rest of us. And Andrew, who looks about as comfortable swinging a golf club as would a squid, is staying inadvertently faithful to his two-bad-shots-per-one-good pattern. All of this helps my frame of mind.

What's more, my aggravation need last only a week: we're scheduled to tee it up again the following Saturday for a friendly round of skins.

On that morning, another stunner, Rob and I share a pre-round pail while Dave and Andrew do the same. This time I abandon any thoughts of a fine-tuning miracle. I merely want to enjoy the sunshine with my boyhood pals and perhaps produce a few good clicks along the way.

While exchanging chitchat and smacking some mid-irons, I accidentally notice something about my swing, something that's making my shots unusually crisp. Investigating this development with the 3-iron, I try a few more. Soon I realize I'm keeping my hands forward, just slightly. It's a simple move, but the ramifications are momentous. So many years and so many rounds, and this seems to have been the secret all along. I apply the technique to my wedges—it works!—and then to my woods—works again! The trajectory of every shot is like a perfect rainbow drawn by a sure hand, and the secret I've stumbled upon is the pot of gold at the end of it.

I look down, concealing a grin. The others don't know it, but they're in trouble today.

Young Drivers

I grew up idolizing men who could swing a baseball bat like a finely calibrated whip, hockey players who could fire a puck into the top corner of the net with an imperceptible snap of the wrists and basketball players who seemed to hang in the air even as I did my business in the bathroom and returned.

Golf was a game played by oddly dressed men whose paunches resembled my father's. At best a harmless pursuit for those who could no longer undertake serious athletics, it occupied a realm well below those sports I loved, sports in which balls were constantly in motion up and down a field, back and forth across a net or arcing toward a hoop.

Then, one Saturday when I was fifteen, Dave, Rob, Andrew and I decided to tackle a local golf course as a way to channel our raging hormones in a legally acceptable fashion. By the third hole, I was hooked, compelled by the serene magic of the ball resting on the grass, so full of promise, so vibrant with possibility.

Whatever would happen to that ball was entirely up to me. The pull was irresistible.

The generation after mine has, seemingly in one continuous wave, been ensnared by the same quiet thrill. More accurately, they've fallen in two waves: first, the one inspired by Tiger Woods, carrying along virtually every male big enough to hold a club; and second, the one inspired by Michelle Wie, sending droves of young girls to the range as though they've woken out of a collective trance to realize their destiny is the LPGA.

To plumb this phenomenon more deeply, I decide to play a round with two of my wife's younger cousins. Fifteen-year-old Jeremy, who barely reached my chin last summer and now faces me at eye level, has transformed from a tentative, innocent boy into a strapping young man full of confidence and roguish charm. His younger brother, Daniel, already an accomplished tennis player at thirteen, exudes more poise and depth than I did at twenty, but at least his driver has a Popeye headcover. I'll still be able to relate.

Riding toward the first tee, I ask Jeremy to name his favorite golfer.

"Tiger."

"Why?"

"I don't know. You gonna edit this?"

"What is it you like about him?"

"He's cool."

"Compared to whom?"

"The white golfers."

I suspend the interrogation long enough to watch Jeremy launch a majestic 3-wood down the center of the fairway with as little effort as it takes to flick an ant off one's knee. When he returns to the cart, I ask him how many lessons he's taken.

Maybe five, he says. This doesn't satisfactorily explain why his swing looks like a beautifully uncoiling serpent and mine like that of a junior woodsman.

Daniel is up next. His still-young muscles, not having learned to trust the slingshot effect of a golf swing, do not yet flash the club the way his older brother's do, but it matters little, because in his more deliberate stroke there are the patience and fluidity that have never even visited mine. Like Jeremy, Daniel ends up mid-fairway.

Barry, the boys' dad, thankfully plays at my level, his floppy, homemade, off-the-back-foot swing a flailing scarecrow to my thrashing lumberjack. On the second hole, Barry attempts to blast out of a fairway bunker and instead catches the lip, somehow snapping the head clean off his 7-iron. Moments later, attempting to curve a 5-wood around a tree and down the fairway, I send my ball into the tops of some maples, which surely laugh their foliage off the instant I turn away.

On the third, I manage par; on the fourth, falsely encouraged, I try to hit my tee shot 800 yards and instead ring the ball off a chainlink fence just to the right of the tee. Though the ball kindly ricochets back toward the tee blocks, the hole remains the same 529 yards away it was before. So, on the next shot, instead of trying to hit it 800 yards, I do the intelligent thing and try to hit it six miles. The ball goes slicing into infinity faster than you can say *penalty stroke*.

"How does it make you feel inside when you strike the ball cleanly?" I ask Daniel as we approach the next tee.

"Good. Strong."

"How would you characterize my swing?"

"Pretty weird."

"Do you feel my slice is average, above-average or inconceivable?"

"The last one. Hey, can you call me Weiner Nunez in the article instead of Daniel Goldlist?"

On the 135-yard fifth, Jeremy momentarily considers a 9-iron, then opts for a wedge, landing the ball within a few feet of the hole. But a soft putting touch has not yet caught up with his burgeoning power; he slides the birdie attempt long, prompting him for some reason to accuse Daniel of being a moron.

"You're a loser," Daniel replies.

"You're a double loser."

"You suck."

"You suck more."

As I'm about to tee off on the sixth, Jeremy exclaims, "Hey, this is the hole where Dad got hit in the ass!" He and Daniel break into hysterics while Barry relates to me the true story of a ball soaring over the rear fairway and caroming off his left buttock.

I re-evaluate my tee shot while Jeremy and Daniel hurl grass in each other's faces and exchange insults regarding various forms of mental deficiency. Staring outward, I realize I have no idea what I'm considering: the hole is a 365-yard dogleg around a gargantuan lake on the right, the kind of hole that makes me start sweating, if not weeping aloud. My only option is to aim the ball directly at the lake and hope it swerves back onto the fairway. Overcompensating, I end up in a solitary, out-of-the-way bunker the course architect surely added just to see if anyone would ever land in it.

Jeremy waggles a 3-wood briefly, then mashes his drive over the lake and into the trees beyond it. He whirls on Daniel.

"Stop talking! Dad, I can't tee off when Daniel's talking."

"Daniel, stop talking when your brother's teeing off."

"He was talking when I teed off!"

"You're both teeing me off."

I ask Jeremy whether he considers golf a gentleman's game.

"Sure."

"If you could play one professional sport, would it be golf?"

"No, hockey. No, wait, golf."

"Why?"

"Lasts longer."

"What do you think of my swing?"

"I'd call it a power fade."

I promise to buy Jeremy lunch.

On the eighth, Barry tops his drive, skidding the ball along the grass as though a manic gopher were trying to steal it. Barry and I seem to be attempting to outdo each other's comedy. He hooks one into the trees, I slice one into next week; he leaves a putt short, I skate one long; he shanks his drive, I flub my chip. As the boys might state, we suck. Huge.

Curiously, the only thing Barry and I have over the younger two is an equanimity that allows us to maintain a consistent, if poor, level of golf through 18 holes. Following the turn, their youthful blood coursing too hot and too fast, Jeremy and Daniel fight a combined meltdown—the consequence of throwing, or suppressing, too many tantrums—and their games begin to unravel.

There's a cruel irony here. Barry and I boast all the perspective in the world but are missing the talent to do anything with it; Jeremy and Daniel, though possessing boundless ability, lack the levelheadedness to keep it under control. Their biggest challenge is in managing not the course, but themselves.

No matter their spiraling frustration, the boys do have fun ways of venting. A particularly favored game has one flipping tees at the other as he tries to hit. As far as I can tell, points are earned if one can fling the tee precisely enough that it hits the other in the cheek just as he begins his backswing.

"You're mental."

"You're retarded."

"Idiot."

"Girl."

On the fifteenth, Jeremy takes bogey as a result of his drive sailing too far past another dogleg. I take double-bogey as a result of the clubs in my bag still carrying a puzzling vendetta against me. Daniel matches Jeremy's bogey, dropping a nice approach onto the green after hitting into the rough off the tee and fervently proclaiming his hatred of golf, his brother, his father and anyone else who ever lived.

By the par-5 eighteenth, the boys are emotionally depleted, but their raw ability has still generated scores better than either Barry's or mine. If there are any poor-sighted squirrels in the woods mistaking chestnuts for golf balls today, they must think they've hit the jackpot.

Jeremy steps up and, with a swing as easy as a rug unfurling, murders his drive. The ball rolls to within inches of the 150-yard marker. With a mammoth 3-iron, he's just off the green, and then, with a soft chip, on in three. Daniel stays straight and smart, hitting four clean balls to get on as well. Barry's drive ends up in the ravine on the right; mine slices into a hill of wild rough on the left that might as well be molten lava given the likelihood of my getting out of it.

Eventually Barry and I reach the green, where Jeremy and Daniel are exchanging punches and laughter. After we all two-putt, I place both boys in a double headlock to let them know

I'm still cool even if my golf game is harder to watch than Keanu Reeves in *Hamlet*.

In the clubhouse after the round, Jeremy and Daniel make their twin platters of chicken wings, deep-fried shrimp and breaded mozzarella nearly vanish in the time it takes me to eat two strips of grilled turkey.

"So why do you think Tiger's been less dominant lately?" I ask.

"Couldn't tell you," says Jeremy.

"Me either," adds Daniel.

"Do you think it's from switching coaches?"

"Nah."

"Did you know he recently got married to Elin Nordegren?"

"Who?"

"Never mind. Do you think he's distracted? Not focused like before?"

"Uh-uh."

"Bored with winning so often?"

The boys try to compute this idea, but since it barely makes sense to me, why would it make sense to them?

"You're right," I say, "it's always fun to win. What, then?"

Jeremy snatches the last shrimp from his brother's plate, calls him a dork, and says, "Everyone else is just getting better."

Indeed.

A Christmas Miracle

The end of the golf season in Canada, though predictable, remains upsetting in the same way one can anticipate Monday but still feels slighted when it arrives. Still, the shift from warm weather to cold brings with it a distinct vitality, for, as anyone living in a variable climate will tell you, one either celebrates the seasons or moves to Florida.

This spirit, defined by the love of getting a snowball in the face, fuels me as I dash up and down the court during my weekly game of pickup basketball. Andrew, Dave and Rob are here, along with two of Dave's law colleagues, forming a game of three-on-three that would make most decent basketball players cringe.

Nonetheless, we play to win. Sometimes our competitive fire results in injuries typical of working stiffs who attempt to transform into elite athletes for a few hours each week. Tonight the highlight injury is mine, a result of my brain convincing my body to try a new quasi-reverse lay-up while in midair. The outcome is a nasty collision with the wall behind the hoop and Andrew exclaiming, "What in the name of Methuselah was that?" rather than checking to see whether I'm alive.

After the game, pleasurably drained, I head home, my thumbs shamelessly tapping the wheel to Katrina and the Waves. Scanning the scenery, I notice a sign reading MINI-GOLF—YEAR-ROUND. I have a half-hour before Stephanie expects me.

The allure of miniature golf is as strong today as when posters of Christie Brinkley covered every inch of my bedroom wall. Whereas adult courses siphon bits of my self-esteem one tragicomic hole at a time, mini-golf layouts were scenes of frequent triumph for me as a child.

The man at the desk greets me, a puff of steam coming from his mouth. I ask how he manages to maintain an outdoor mini-golf course when winter is wrapping its arms around the entire city.

"I want to make sure people have somewhere to get their fix while waiting for spring. Be conservative at the sixteenth—that windmill's tougher than it looks. Got a driving range out back, by the way."

Holding a putter in one hand and a fluorescent orange golf ball in the other, I'm guided through a door and onto a black mat with three holes. I look up to see a minuscule red-and-white house, beautifully painted, twin tunnels cut through its base. The rest of the course gleams as though hand-crafted hours before.

Somehow the air is warm here; as I retrieve my ball from the first hole after taking a two (okay, three—Bobby Jones couldn't have made that one-footer with the ball sitting against the corner), I remove my hat, scarf and gloves. Though in the distance a blanket of fresh snow is visible, the course itself seems to exist in perpetual July.

Positioning my ball on the mat at the sixteenth, with its menacing windmill, I step back to assess the situation. I'm carding 31—one over—including two aces and three bogeys.

"Take a good look," says a voice. I look up to see a different man, sporting plus fours and a beige tam-o'-shanter. "This hole can make or break the round." His pronunciation of round as *rrrayind* suggests he is either Scottish or has been hypnotized into thinking he is.

"Hi. Have you been playing behind me?"

"Haven't plaiyed ferrr a long taime. Now ay jest watch."

"Watch?"

"Ferrr talent—like yeurs. That swing is rrraw, bayt theire's maigic in it. Aiy'd like te sei ye tike sem biggerrr kets. Shaill we hid to the rrrange?"

"I can see how you'd be impressed by my mini-golf game," I tell him, "but I'm afraid it doesn't quite translate."

"Perrrhaps aiy could be the judge of thait."

The driving range seems plucked from a fairy tale, its yardage signs glittering white against the darkness, its landing areas bottom-lit, emitting a soft glow. The man in the Tam hands me a 5-iron. Only after hitting the ball straight 160 yards do I notice the temperature here is as balmy as it was on the mini-golf course. "How is it kept so warm?" I ask, removing my coat.

"Laiyt's net worry about thait. Aiy believe yerrr rrreidy."

"Ready for what?"

The man snaps his fingers. Suddenly, I am no longer standing at the inexplicably climate-controlled range but between two tee boxes at a course I've never seen.

"May the best man win," says a nasal voice. I look down to see a hand extended, then up to see it's attached to Tiger Woods.

I accept his handshake with the same expression one might have watching a supernova.

"Or woman," says another voice. Babe Didrikson Zaharias grins slyly at Tiger, then winks at me. "You know the only thing tougher than a tiger? A tigress." She starts warming up, her swing as fluid as a waterwheel.

My jaw drops. "Isn't she—"

"Ineligible? Technically, yes," says Tiger, "but they granted her an exemption. Look, you supported it."

"Of course. That is one nice swing."

"She throws a mean javelin, too."

From behind Tiger appears Mark Twain, in white-on-white. His mustache twitches genially in my direction, then in Babe's and, finally, Tiger's. "The aptly named," he chirps at Tiger, raising his chin.

"Mr. Twain?" I say. "What about golf being a good walk spoiled and all that?"

"I desired to see what all the commotion is about. If it must be on the golf course, then on the golf course it must be."

A microphone is thrust in my face and a man with a toupee like a flattened gerbil says, "I'm here with the reigning king of golf, I.J. Schecter. I.J., by now the story of your endless hours at the range even in mid-winter is well known. Can you tell us whether it's also true that you originally polished your stroke on mini-golf courses?"

"Wherever it was," Tiger says, leaning in, "it worked. He really came out of nowhere."

"Quite," says Twain, arching an eyebrow.

"What's your plan today?" the reporter asks Tiger.

"Well, there are three of us and one of him, so I'm hoping we can grab a few before he gets into one of those grooves."

"What tournament is this?" I ask.

The reporter turns toward a second camera. "What tournament is this! That kind of ability and a sense of humor to match!" Twain is eyeing me suspiciously. I want to tell him he's been dead nearly a century, but I'm too worried he'll come up with something clever in response. "All right, viewers, we're just about ready to kick off the first-ever three-on-one skins match. To remind you, I.J. Schecter will take on three competitors at once. If any of their scores are better than his on a given hole, they take the skin. If his score is better than the other three, the skin is his."

"Ladies and gentlemen," says another voice, "on the tee, I.J." Thrilled I've achieved single-name celebrity status alongside Tiger, Vijay, Sergio and Britney, I push my tee and Top-Flite Hot XL into the ground. A lovely calm ripples through me as my fingers settle onto the shaft as though gently grasping my wife's foot for a massage. In an unbending triangle my arms and hands lift backward; my hips turn as easily as those of a salsa instructor; my wrists hinge, activating a silent button; then it all unleashes, and I feel my muscles working in harmony as never before, a flawlessly calibrated slingshot.

My swing whizzes through like it's following the edge of a gyroscope—smooth, even, unhurried. I observe the pretty arc of the shot, my pulse as relaxed as if I were watering the lawn. The ball leaps off my club and down the fairway, anxious to see what's out there. This is a surprise to me, since my drives are usually scared stiff of fairways.

The match proceeds heavily in my favor, Tiger and Babe unnerved by my shot-making and Twain—though you have to watch what you say around him—nubbing his shots harmlessly forward and saying things like "That ball ought to find better things to do" or "There are those who enjoy golf, and then there are the sane."

Through seventeen holes, I've won all but three skins. The fifth hole, designated an automatic win for the other side if I didn't ace it (since I'd apparently accomplished the feat twice this year) was a near-miss, my 8-iron landing four inches from the cup. At the tenth, a severe side cramp during my backswing, a result of downing two hot dogs and a Gatorade at the turn, allowed Babe to steal one for them with an up-and-down that would make most golfers curl into the fetal position. And, from the gallery on 15, Tiger's wife, the former Ms. Nordegren, flashed me a smile that—I'm sure I didn't imagine this—was like an invitation to review her course architecture. Spraying the ball left and right, I carded eight, re-focusing in time to eagle the next two holes.

The narrow fairway at 18 requires a precise draw off the tee. Though I can't remember having hit a draw in my life—not intentionally, at least—today I've been executing them with as little difficulty as it takes to breathe. Feeling like I was born with a driver in my hands I pull back the club, arms and hands maintaining the same wonderful triangle rather than collapsing into the usual trapezoid. My hips slide forward and, as though attached by an invisible string, pull the rest of my body through.

As the club comes sweeping down, I notice, out of the corner of my eye, Mrs. Woods blowing me a kiss. It's enough to throw me off just slightly. The ball jumps off the heel of my driver, hitting the tee block and ricocheting back toward my forehead. I wonder if Tiger told her to play these head games with me. We all know how much he hates to lo—

"Wake up, Skeeter." The voice sounds like Dave's, though I don't remember seeing him in the gallery. His features, blurry at first, become clear. "We still have the court for an hour." He pulls me up from the floor, shoves the basketball into my hands and slaps me on the shoulder. "Awesome wipeout. You really taught that wall a lesson."

An hour later, I'm announcing to Stephanie both that I'm home and that it still looks as though I'll never play pro basketball. She plants a warm kiss on my stubble, squeezes my arm and asks how the game was tonight.

"A dream."

With Resolve

Though forever ready to make impassioned New Year's resolutions, I've never been good at keeping them. There was the pledge to learn how to make a meal other than macaroni, which resulted only in learning how to make spaghetti; the one about going to the gym three times per week, which became inventing three lame excuses per week instead; and the reckless ninth-grade pledge to kiss Amanda Green, a foolish declaration since I've always lacked touch around the greens.

So when it came my turn around the table to state my ambition for the year ahead, I was quite troubled to hear my mouth utter the words "Break a hundred." My dinner companions, all of whom had offered resolutions as dull as they were safe (tend to the lawn more often, be more forthcoming with charitable dollars, read a novel once in a blue moon) looked at me as though I'd declared I was going to climb Mount Everest with a pogo stick.

This may have been because they were remembering my previous New Year's resolution—to banish my slice to purgatory, or at least to some other golfer—which had gone less than swimmingly.

I'd thought my plan was sound. Asking myself to improve on the links without assistance would be about as fair as asking an elk to fly, so unorthodox help had seemed in order. My first step, in early February, was a visit to the acupuncturist.

The nameplate on the office door, Dr. Les Hook, told me immediately I'd made a good choice. Anyone who could lessen a hook could surely reduce a slice. Dr. Hook explained that his technique was based on the ancient Chinese belief in the body's vital energy circulating through channels that could sometimes fall out of kilter. Though I admittedly tuned him out between the words "ancient" and "kilter," instead replaying in my head the one clean 5-wood I'd hit the previous season, he seemed rational enough.

By inserting a number of stainless steel needles into my body and sending a low-frequency current through them, described Dr. Hook, he hoped to restore my imbalance. Whatever turns you on, I said, hoping he was better with stainless steel than I was with irons. Do away with the slice and I'll make acupuncture my religion.

Minutes later I felt like a human golf ball, dimples replaced with needles. Dr. Hook left the room as I watched little muscles all over my body jump and quiver, probably as excited as I was at the thought of losing the slice.

Some weeks later, the ground thawed, my snow shovel consigned to storage for another year, I struck out for the links. My slice was even more awe-inspiring than usual. I spent the entire round punching out of the woods or unzipping the pocket of my bag for replacement Titleists. Though I recorded only the third-worst score of our foursome (the fourth being my twelve-year-old cousin Kate), I left the course feeling violently non-religious about acupuncture.

Steadfast, I made the next obvious choice to improve my golf game: hypnosis. Entering the office of Dr. Carrie Lake (another promising name), I asked whether she was going to put me in a trance and install a microchip in my forehead that prevented a golf ball from finding water.

"'Trance' is a misleading term," said Dr. Lake, her expression implying that humor and hypnosis did not belong in the same room. "Nothing about your conscious state is altered under hypersuggestion."

"Hypersuggestion? I thought it was hypnosis."

"Let us call it hypnotic suggestibility."

"Just to be clear, I don't want the one where my slice disappears for a year and then comes back. I want the permanent one, even if it costs more."

Dr. Lake cleared her throat. "I'm going to induce an extremely relaxed state, followed by the suggestion of certain motor activities."

"A relaxed state is a good start. Usually I grip the shaft so tight my knuckles turn whi—"

"Shall we begin?"

Over the course of the next half-hour, Dr. Lake gave me a series of instructions in a soothing, unhurried voice, the kind of voice that would work well as a golf stroke. I kept expecting her to swing a watch back and forth in front of my eyes and tell me I was getting very sleepy, but instead she just talked, ever so slowly, ever so calmly, until an hour had elapsed, whereupon her normal voice returned, more like that of a canary with bronchitis.

She told me we were done—again I was disappointed, having expected a finger-snap that would jolt me out of my fugue and propel me to the nearest course to shoot in the 70s—and asked whether I'd like to pay via check or cash. Assuming I wasn't still hypnotized, I passed the money across the table and thanked her for suggesting to my body how to play golf properly.

Tackling the same 18 holes that afternoon to ensure the suggestion wouldn't accidentally slip out of my brain overnight, I proceeded to take divots the size of landing strips and pound my drives so far off-line that the trees didn't even seem interested in trying to snare them. I departed the course feeling about hypnosis approximately the way I did about acupuncture, although, curiously, my usual post-round chocolate chip ice cream craving had disappeared.

Failed by both acupuncture and hypnosis, I turned to the method that should have been obvious all along: chakra alignment. Having undergone the procedure months before, my friend Glen assured me it had brought all the parts of his body into lovely alignment. I asked him if he thought it would help my golf game. He told me two things: one, that nothing was likely to help my game, though if anything could, this was it; and two, even if it didn't get rid of my slice, it would guarantee me more powerful orgasms.

I visited Glen's chakra expert, a woman called Zenith working out of a basement apartment that, after I entered through a doorway of hanging beads, announced itself via the scent of jasmine and tulips, or maybe just cheap perfume.

Zenith explained that chakras are, according to Tantric philosophy, points of energy in the astral body. Though unnerved by the mention of Tantric philosophy because I'd heard of it only as a tool for Sting to have mind-blowing sex, I hung around. Perhaps Sting and Glen simply owned the same reading materials.

There are seven primary chakras, said Zenith, each associated with various emotions, desires and powers. I asked her which one was associated with fairways. She smiled in tranquil amusement and requested that I step behind a curtain, remove my clothes and enter the bath that had been prepared. Though the principles behind chakra alignment sounded suspiciously like those governing acupuncture, I felt desperate to eradicate the slice. Also, who can refuse a bubble bath?

Zenith told me to breathe in through my nose and out through my mouth three times. I did this and asked if my game had been fixed. She told me to picture the white light of God and of universal love swirling around me counterclockwise. I could have sworn the white light of universal love would move clockwise, but, dying to rid myself of the thorn that had attached itself to me as cheerfully as an oxpecker to a hippopotamus, I complied.

I was then told to picture a purple light swirling around my head counterclockwise. If it felt hard to mentally move the light around, said Zenith, I was permitted to try it clockwise. I knew it!

Moments later Zenith informed me we had succeeded in balancing one chakra. Following her direction, I performed similar exercises with my forehead (indigo light), throat (blue), chest (pink or, if I preferred, green—nice to have options), solar plexus (yellow), belly (orange) and pelvis (red). After toweling off and pushing my way back through the beads, I made for the nearest course, clubs in hand.

It seemed Zenith had succeeded not in aligning my chakras but in reconfiguring their crookedness. My slice had simply mutated, transforming from a horizontal parabola into a shape that looked like a question mark drawn by someone tripping on acid.

Nearly out of options, I found myself browsing a random golf website and an item resembling a falconer's glove named ... let's call it the Grip Stabilizer 3000 (Grip Stabilizer because it sounds plausible, 3000 because it seems to adorn every new product that appears on the market—Garden Rake 3000, Veg-O-Matic 3000, Nose Hair Trimmer 3000). In the online demo, a charming lunk-head from somewhere in the southern U.S. promised me this product would ensure my hands were at or ahead of the ball at impact. The accompanying ad hollered confidently, *Solid at Impact Means Longer Off the Tee!* and, just beneath, *HELPS YOU KEEP IT FIRM!*

Unsure whether I was purchasing a golf tool or sexual aid, I clicked "Add to Cart," and the miracle invention arrived at my doorstep a mere three weeks later.

Apparently, the designers of the Grip Stabilizer 3000, though dedicated to making sure my front hand remained straight, were unconcerned about my back arm flying outward as though I were half-man, half-chicken. The Grip Stabilizer 3000, like acu-puncture, hypnotic suggestion and chakra alignment before it, succeeded in eliminating not a fraction of my slice, and made me look like a certified nut to boot. To the makers of Grip Stabilizer 3000 I have this to say: Fool me once, shame on you. Fool me twice, and I'm coming after you with an 8-iron.

Ruing my second consecutive year of liquor-induced idiocy, I gazed around the table at my friends, whom, having just heard me pledge to break a hundred, gazed back the way one might regard a toddler who has vowed to master Tchaikovsky. My friend Jim asked, "How do you plan to get that done, my man?"

Having been failed the year before by the existential route, not to mention the falconer's glove posing as a golf aid, I experienced a mini-revelation. A course of action occurred to me that I'd never before considered, an idea so outlandish, a scheme so ludicrous, that it just might work. I could seek professional instruction. Then I thought better of the idea, instead choosing the much nobler, and much more moronic, path of working the problems out on my own.

"By sheer force of will, Jim," I smiled. "Eventually the bad habits have to give way to some good ones."

Jim looked at me, perplexed. Even I didn't know what I'd meant. Everyone knows that the trench dug by bad golf habits can become bottomless if those habits aren't grabbed by the collar and slowly reversed.

"Sounds like the champagne talking," Jim said.

"Indeed," I smiled, aware of my incoherence but somehow impressed with myself.

We toasted over the clink of glasses, tipped champagne flutes against our lips and sang "Auld Lang Syne." All the while, I tingled with anticipation. The only thing left to do was wait for spring.

Ten Reasons I'll (Probably) Never Take a Golf Lesson

Would taking a few golf lessons improve my game? Probably. Would it enhance my golf experience? Of course not. Here are ten reasons why:

1. **Everyone wants me in his foursome.** Golf is tense at the best of times. I come up with at least two shots per round that throw everyone into hysterics, making me an immensely popular playing partner.

2. **I don't need to study my mechanics.** Sound golfers agonize over why they're not breaking 80 even when their swing feels right. I never have to worry about my swing, because any one of its flaws might be responsible on a given day.

3. **I never have to make excuses.** When a good golfer shanks one, he is obligated to stare at the club, act bewildered and say

something like, "Caught too much grass," "Hit it off the toe" or "I don't understand, I usually hit my 3-wood exactly 200." When I hit a 3-wood 200 yards, I simply say, "Pure luck," and move on.

4. **Strategy is irrelevant.** I don't have to worry about draws, fades, pitch-and-runs, bunker saves or reading greens. My strategy is always the same: swing hard and pray like hell.

5. **It's easy for me to impress myself.** The pleasure I get from hitting a ball cleanly is unmitigated since it happens so infrequently. Good players barely react after hitting one solid because they're only meeting their own expectations.

6. **A miracle round is always right around the corner.** Consistent players spend years just trying to shave a stroke or two. All I need is one day when it all accidentally comes together and I might take ten strokes off faster than you can say Jose Maria Olazabal. Sure, it hasn't happened yet, but the point is that it could.

7. **My bag doesn't contain more metal than a Buick.** Unlike more refined players, I have no need for a 1-iron, 7-wood, lob wedge, two drivers and three putters, because the path of my shot has little to do with the club I'm using. The only true essentials in my bag are a ball retriever and a sand wedge.

8. **Shotmaking is my specialty—in fact, no two shots ever look the same.** The many different trajectories my shots take keep the game interesting. At any moment, I might unleash the

Colossal Slice, the Worm Burner, the Major League Pop-Up, the Ripple Maker or the Game-Winning Double Down the Line. If I took enough lessons, my shots would all start to look the same. How boring would that be?

9. **I have no illusions about my game.** The more talented a golfer becomes, the more likely he is to start thinking he might actually become good enough one day to crack the tour. I'm happy just to sink a five-foot putt.

10. **I get more bang for my buck.** For me, a 50-dollar round means two strokes per dollar—more if I'm not on my game. A golfer who cards 85 has taken a mere 1.7 shots for every dollar. So who gets more out of an average round?

Uncle Hugh's Rules for Maintaining a Ten Handicap

Natural athletic ability, we all know, correlates with good golf about as much as Christina Aguilera correlates with good taste. Each of us has a friend who, despite being able to handle a baseball bat with aplomb, sink two free throws when it counts or execute a half-volley, couldn't hit an approach from 80 yards to save his life.

Conversely, each of us also knows one or two individuals prone to walking into doors who somehow become marvels of coordination the moment they pick up a golf club. This is because the golf swing cannot be mastered merely through extrapolation of general physical talent. If you can play basketball, you can probably play some tennis. If you can handle yourself reasonably on a tennis court, it's a decent bet you can do the same on a baseball diamond. From baseball you can transfer a certain amount of skill to volleyball, from volleyball to football, and so on. But not one of these pursuits, nor any of their cousins, can help you hit a 2-iron. Attempting to reapply one to the other can, in fact, prove disastrous (to you, at least. It's probably a scream to your playing partners. I wish I had a dollar for every time I've heard one of my friends say, "There's another beautiful baseball swing. Too bad we're playing golf.") Yes, golf is its own unique beast, and there's no predicting who can tame it and who can't.

That said, I've always been suspicious of my uncle Hugh. Though he's in his mid-fifties, carries 30 extra pounds and walks like a mule with a double hernia, he claims a ten handicap. Recently I decided to play a round with Uncle Hugh to uncover his secrets. Rounding out our foursome were his wife, my aunt Vivian, an attorney who would rather card 180 than break a rule, and my friend Mitchell, who prefers to be called "The Masher" as a way of compensating for having never hit a respectable 3-wood in his life.

On the first hole, Uncle Hugh whistles his drive into the next county, says "Mully," and immediately tees up another. Though I make it a rule never to use mulligans—mostly because there's no reason to believe my second shot will be any better than my first—the majority of golfers consider them the one acceptable pardon in a game otherwise as merciful as Attila the Hun. So I don't count this against Uncle Hugh's score. It's when he uses mulligans on the next three holes that I start counting.

On the fifth, Uncle Hugh attempts a 7-wood from the left half of the fairway and promptly sends his Hot Core Maxfli on a trajectory similar to that of an inebriated planet. "Yep," says Uncle Hugh, removing a new ball and substituting a mid-iron for the 7-wood, "coulda told you I was gonna slice that son of a bitch before I took it out of the bag."

The score Uncle Hugh reports at the end of the hole curiously omits his delinquent 7-wood as well as its attendant penalty stroke. Thus is revealed one of the rules underlying Uncle Hugh's formidable game: If the only purpose of a shot was to confirm you can't hit a certain club, it shouldn't count. (A school companion of mine used to use similar logic. Studying for his exams, he declared, was a waste of time because he knew he was going to fail anyway. When he did inevitably fail, his point was proven. Who could argue?)

As we make our way to the eighth, Uncle Hugh proves shrewder than I'd originally thought. Mitchell, official scorer for the round, has just three-putted at the sixth. His anguish is transparent, and also pitiable in a glad-it-wasn't-me sort of way. Uncle Hugh chooses this moment to note that he scored five on the previous hole. Though I know it was a six, Mitchell records the five unconsciously, oblivious to everything but the mental tape of his three-putt cruelly rewinding. This technique of Uncle Hugh's is deceptively simple: mention your score on a given hole when your playing partners are consumed by their own ineptness. Later, after Mitchell four-putts the thirteenth and Uncle Hugh says, "Another bird," he might as well be saying, "There's a stegosaurus."

At the ninth, with his ball resting against the base of a tree, Uncle Hugh announces that one is allowed to move his ball one club length if it is obstructed by a tree shorter than six feet. Neither I nor Aunt Viv nor Mitchell argues—mostly because we're all trying to figure out exactly which tree Uncle Hugh is referring to. It couldn't be the one blocking his ball, since that tree is about twice Uncle Hugh's height, and surely he realizes he is over three feet tall. Another of the tenets in Uncle Hugh's guidebook surfaces: If you aren't happy with the spot where your ball lands, you are permitted to interpret a rule in a manner ludicrous enough that your playing partners would rather have you move the ball than engage in a debate that would insult the intelligence of *Homo erectus*. Uncle Hugh kicks his ball about four club lengths away from the tree. His arsenal is impressive indeed.

As we near the turn, with my game unraveling quickly, Aunt Viv spending most of the round on her cell phone and Mitchell the Masher ready to sell his soul for a two-putt, Uncle Hugh catches a pretty 6-iron that leaves him a downhill seven-footer for even. He strolls onto the green, assesses the line, then scoops up his ball and says, "I'll take a par."

This intrigues me. You can't just *take* a par; you have to earn one. In any case, Uncle Hugh has made it plain that he considers this putt, which would make most people drop their bag and sprint in the other direction, automatic. We all have our specialty shots, I suppose. Perhaps Uncle Hugh is buying into the delusion that if you've made a shot once, it's at least a hypothetical possibility that you'll make it every time. If he has made one downhill seven-footer in his life, there is therefore no reason not to pick up this putt. Next time I have a 190-yard approach into a crosswind, I'll pick up my ball, too, citing the one miracle 3-wood I hit 12 years ago.

When Uncle Hugh comes up short on the water-guarded par-3 twelfth, he takes his drop on the side of the pond nearest the green, despite the rulebook's fairly clear view on this. Thus lying two, he places his ball just off the fringe. I mentally note another of his statutes: the location of a drop is in the eye of the beholder.

At the sixteenth, Uncle Hugh botches his second shot, a rash 4-iron from the rough as high as my ankles. He looks at the club in utter bafflement, like a tennis player searching for the hole in his racket. It's as though his brain is trying to compute data it can't handle. Uncle Hugh's bewilderment represents the paradox faced by every recreational golfer. Why, if we choose the right club and take the right swing, does the ball still end up in such unwelcome places? The answer, of course, is that we seldom take the right swing.

Uncle Hugh drops a new ball in the same spot. Well, not quite the same spot—more like ten yards up and five yards onto the fairway. Another of his rules emerges: If you thought everything about your swing was right, and it still went wrong, you really ought not to be penalized.

Like any great performer, Uncle Hugh leaves the best for last. At 18 he invokes the golf equivalent of *abracadabra*, the magical incantation that immutably changes one's score forever. When Mitchell asks Uncle Hugh his score, he replies, "Gimme a five," and suddenly the three shots he took to get to the bunker, as well as the two he took to get out, are erased. Uncle Hugh isn't technically lying or cheating. He's merely choosing to answer the question "What would you like to have gotten?" instead of "What did you get?" I'd be inclined to take up this semantic question with Aunt Viv if she didn't look like she wanted to bury her head in the sand.

Over a beer in the clubhouse Mitchell announces the final tallies for the round, including Uncle Hugh's 85. When Uncle Hugh excuses himself for a moment, the Masher leans toward me and murmurs, "Or 103, if you live in the real world." I'm not sure whether the 103 is exact—for most of the back nine, Mitch looked like a rabid dog ready to strike—but the precise number matters little. Uncle Hugh has eliminated somewhere in the neighborhood of 18 strokes. Aunt Viv finishes at 106, the Masher at 112. My own score is 110—but it's an honest 110, and honesty is all one can ask for. (I suppose one could also ask for a short game, but that doesn't appear to be in the cards, so honesty will have to suffice.)

A few minutes later, listening to Uncle Hugh describe his eagle on 11—indeed it would have been an eagle, were the hole a par 7—I feel I've accomplished something important today, something crucial to the duffer's self-worth. While I don't feel any better about my own game, I certainly feel a lot better about his.

Forces of Nature

Whether I can actually hear the distant thunder of Niagara Falls or whether I only believe I can, I'm not certain. But real or imaginary, I know I'd better shake the thought if I'm going to play half-respectably today. Thinking about the Falls is like thinking about highways being built to span entire countries or newspapers some-how getting written, printed and distributed to millions of people every morning—the concepts are too large. My mind, of which I apparently only manage to use a small part, needs time to work things out. It takes an hour just to complete the head-shaking phase in which all I'm saying to the next person is "That's unbelievable." Having passed the awestruck stage, I find myself unsettled to learn that my brain wishes to explore the topic further. The prospect is troubling; I'm going to be forced to consider the details of how such things occur. Like tackling the big questions (*Why are we here? Are we alone? Will anyone ever break DiMaggio's streak?*), such men-tal pursuits are both exciting and intimidating, drawing us toward them even as we realize we may derive nothing other than the feeling of mental shortage. Eventually we go back to whatever we were thinking about before going down this path, simpler matters one barely need be conscious to examine, like absently inspecting the length of his fingernails or trying to figure out when he started favoring black licorice over red.

"You going to hit?" asks Andrew.

We're standing on the first tee at Royal Niagara. It's a perfect July morning, and I'm standing between two tee blocks as unfocused as if the *Sports Illustrated* swimsuit shoot were occurring behind me. Nestled between the historic 120-year-old Welland Canal, the gorgeous Bruce Trail and the Niagara Escarpment, and measuring over 7,000 yards from the tips, Royal Niagara offers visual pleasures in abundance, from impeccable fairways to cavernous bunkers to gleaming water. But all I can think about is the Falls and the volume of water plummeting over that crest, one moment part of Lake Erie, the next snatched down into the foam.

"Give me a minute," I reply, trying to shake the Falls from my mind. At Royal Niagara there are three nine-hole offerings: the Escarpment Course, which runs south to the base of the wooded escarpment, swings upward toward its summit, then returns downhill past the central pond; the water-dominated Old Canal Course; and the Iron Bridge Course, whose first three holes run diagonal across the property to the eponymous iron bridge before arriving at the abandoned tunnel entrance, where, I suppose, golfers in the middle of an especially bad round can simply curl up and await the comfort of death.

We've chosen to begin with the Escarpment Course and have decided to play its blue tees, since the landscape before us seems, for the most part, unthreatening. Hardly a hazard can be seen between us and the flag over 400 yards away, unless you count as hazards the 36-wheelers rumbling along the Queen Elizabeth Way above the left side of the fairway.

Nerves jumping, I assume I'm going to whistle one right, slice it back toward the freeway and hit the windshield of a semi. To worsen matters, I'm wearing a yellow golf shirt—a mandatory outfit choice, since it was a gift from Stephanie—for the first time in my golfing life, highlighted thus far by safe earth tones and the occasional conservative splash of blue. The little green alligator on my chest is making me doubly self-conscious. Steph says this look is in, but all I can think about is how nerdy I felt wearing it two decades ago in eighth grade. How can it make me look cool now?

"Skeeter?"

"Right—sorry." I decided long ago to give myself over to Steph's knowledge of fashion. I have to forget about the alligator and the bold statement of yellow and simply focus on golf. I stand at address, imagine a gigantic drive, subtract the slice from the mental image, then pull the trigger.

The good news is I don't slice the ball at all; the bad news is I lift my head early and hit the ball off the heel. Rob, Andrew and Dave watch the ball carom off my golf cart and back onto the fairway.

"Designed play?" asks Andrew.

Rob steps up next and pops his drive about 80 yards. Andrew sails his into a fairway bunker on the left. Dave scalds his down the middle, prompting the other three of us to debate whether it really makes sense to be his friend.

"If that's how you're going to play, why don't you join another group?" Rob says.

On the second hole I bend my drive far right, then back into the middle of the fairway. Sadly, my second shot, a 5-iron, fails to understand my instruction to fade and instead slices into the trees on the left, forcing me into one of those dreadful walks where one thrashes among the bushes, half-heartedly searching for his ball as the three others stroll happily toward their within-bounds shots. I find a ball that isn't mine, then another, also not mine. With each sighting of a white crescent poking out from between the twigs and leaves, hope swells in me, then dies just as quickly when I see a Top-Flite or Titleist logo instead of the cursed Pinnacle 3 I'm playing.

Finding a ball that isn't yours is a curiously hurtful experience. Financially speaking, you're happy to replace the one you've lost, but the found ball also serves as a taunting reminder that you'll probably never see the original again and instead must settle for a ball that has merely behaved poorly for some other golfer. Every golfer is connected to every other through this cycle: we abandon a ball for someone else to find; we find a ball someone else has abandoned. The only winners are the balls themselves, who get to witness the comedy stylings of dozens of different golfers over the course of a season.

At the Escarpment third, Rob helps distract me from the hideousness of my game by skulling his drive into some high grass left of the fairway and cursing wildly, not to mention impressively, using about six variations of the same expletive. He then asks to borrow Dave's new Big Bertha driver, whose head seems about the size of an ostrich egg.

After pummeling the spontaneous mulligan down the right side of the fairway, Rob offers Dave 200 dollars for the club. Dave says he'll consider it. On the next hole, using the Big Bertha again and wanting to see just how far he can mash it, Rob overswings, topping the ball and bouncing it pitifully forward. He informs Dave the price has just dropped to 50 bucks. No deal, says Dave.

On the same hole, I somehow manage par by stringing together a decent drive, a lucky 5-wood, a delicate sand wedge—which, through some act of divine clemency, I suddenly know how to hit today—and a ten-foot putt.

The sand wedge revelation is momentous. It seems that, by the simple act of keeping my front forearm stiff, I'm able to control this club, which is usually so disobedient by the turn that I end up stuffing it into my bag for good. If I can control my sand wedge, that means I'm in line to shave several strokes today. So far I've taken three shots with the suddenly cooperative club, and all have landed within 20 feet of the flag. Errant drives aside, maybe this is my day.

Superficially, at least, Royal Niagara would indeed seem ripe for the picking. Despite an acceptable complement of narrow fairways, treacherous bunkers and water that seems equipped with tractor beams, Royal Niagara doesn't issue too deep a panic.

What it doesn't reveal at first blush, however, is a subtler evil that runs throughout the course: fescue. The wild child of golf course design, fescue, a blanched, yellowish, threadlike high grass, looks harmless, yet to say it conceals golf balls effectively is like saying a chameleon has only a moderate chance of winning the average game of hide-and-seek. Hit a perfect drive at Royal Niagara and you're in the fairway imagining par, perhaps even birdie. Hit the same drive just left or right and, more often than not, you end up on a long, ultimately fruitless search through a mass of yellow strands that suddenly make poison ivy seem like tulips.

The ubiquitous fescue exerts a potent psychological effect, as well. There are few things more aggravating to the recreational golfer than hammering an almost-ideal drive yet not being able to find his ball. At Royal Niagara, balls that stray slightly from the fairway become impossible to unearth among the untamed fescue so that, after eight or nine holes, you come to imagine it cackling as it snares yet another ball and your mind lurches a step closer toward madness.

The breeze that picks up around the fifth doesn't help matters. My drive swerves left and lands in a swath of rough between the cart path and the fairway. Trying to hit my second shot, a 3-wood, into next week, I instead bounce it across the fairway and into the rough on the opposite side. I strike my third shot, a 4-iron, surprisingly clean and long—too long, back across the fairway to the rough on the left edge again. I'm lying three and barely threatening the green, but I can't pretend I'm not at least pleasantly surprised to find I can hit a 4-iron.

By thinking about the breeze, however, I've inadvertently resumed thinking about nature and the magnificent playground it has made of this area over so many eons. I contemplate the collisions that have crunched together these rocks, pushing the Escarpment up out of the ground. I realize I've never thought about the fact that the slender club in my grasp is a result of metals being battered within the earth's layers until extracted by humans. It's an embarrassing flaw of the members of modern society that we use and consume so many things yet think so little about the fact that most of them are produced within the depths of the very planet we walk upo—

"Skeeter, if you're waiting for the breeze to die down, you're going to be waiting a long time."

Royal Niagara's signature hole is number six on the Escarpment Nine. The ball is teed up beside me. I look out at the handsome skyline of deep green foliage, and, tucked among it, the old iron bridge, and then I turn to see Rob, Dave and Andrew leaning on their clubs and staring at me.

"Sorry, boys. Here we go."

Thinking too much about the view and not enough about the golf ball I'm trying to sock, I send a weak drive fluttering toward the fairway that dies a 120 yards out like a bird suddenly shot in midair. After Rob sends his drive left and Dave sends his right, Andrew catches one nicely, satisfying the typical one-solid-drive-out-of-four ratio we typically achieve as a group. With his second shot, Andrew succumbs to an even more prevalent tendency, producing a dreadful, unmistakable *THWOP!* that signifies the only shot more injurious to a golfer's soul than a missed putt: the duffed 3-wood.

Esthetically speaking, a missed putt is disappointing, but not devastating. The ball's motion merely continues a bit too long, not quite long enough, or veers too far right or left. But the imagined potential of the 3-wood being so immense, the contrast between the flight path we envision during the backswing and the flub that often results can ravage one's mental faculties. When the woman you worship tells you she just wants to be friends, you're stung at first, but you heal. When a colleague gets promoted ahead of you, you seethe briefly before eventually deciding to work even harder. But a shanked 3-wood is forever. Adding insult to injury, Andrew's flub lands in a patch of fescue 40 yards ahead and somehow vanishes.

Managing to stay focused for a few holes, I produce three consecutive bogeys. Bogeys are all I ever aspire toward on a golf course. Before every round, I convince myself how easy it is to simply play safe and straight, settling for bogeys all the way, since bogey golf all the way means a score of 90. Invariably, a litter of sevens dashes the dream, making me wonder for hours afterward just how I gave away so many shots in so many ways.

As we search for yet another fescue-camouflaged drive on nine, I ask myself how much time we as a group spend looking for balls versus actually hitting them. Someone should paint a portrait of us in this tableau, four figures glancing down into the rough, clubs dangling from our grasps. The painting could be called *Amateur Golf*.

Coming off four poor scores and plenty of fescue-snared balls on the Escarpment Nine, we channel our frustration into cheeseburgers, Gatorades and a heated discussion of where Roger Clemens ranks among all-time pitchers (followed by an even more heated discussion about whether our seventh-grade music teacher, Mrs. Melee, formerly Ms. Wasilenko, was really as hot as we believed at the time) before proceeding to the Old Canal Course. This nine runs along the old Welland Canal, constructed as an intricate lock system in 1829 to link Lake Erie with Lake Ontario, offering ships a safe detour around the Falls.

Stepping up to the first tee, I'm awakened again to the unfathomable processes of geology. I try for the umpteenth time to wrap my mind around the sculpting power of nature, the fact that nothing more than wind and water have carved and re-carved this landscape over billions of years, leaving it as I see it today and as many generations hence will see it.

No earthly process, of course, can compare to the herculean task I have of trying to will this golf ball into the air, which is precisely why I need to forget about wind erosion, tectonic drift and mountain moving. Right now I'll settle for ball moving.

The Old Canal Nine immediately tries to match the deception of the Escarpment Nine, offering us wide-open vistas on the first several holes. We learn quickly not to fall for it. On the Old Canal's second, we hit four clean drives 170 yards into a fairway that we then realize, only upon arriving at our balls, tapers toward the green, causing us to play our second shots blindly into a hidden strip of the canal.

Though the fescue quotient on the Old Canal Nine is much lower than on the Escarpment Nine, this nine has its own wickedness. Old or new, a canal is made of water, and water is as strangely irresistible to the weekend golfer's ball as a terrifying horror movie is to a late-night channel surfer. Here we remain connected to the long line of golfers before us not by losing some balls for others to find and finding some that others have lost but by adding steadily to the collection of balls that have surely accumulated at the bottom of the canal since the day the course opened.

On the Old Canal's third, seeming to forget the trick played on us only a hole earlier, we again relax at the sight of an invitingly wide fairway. This temporary lapse in suspicion kicks off 15 minutes of some of the most improbably bad golf we've ever produced as a group.

Confidence brimming, Rob lashes away with Dave's Big Bertha and sends his ball twisting left into the woods. Realizing the fairway must be narrower than it looks and adjusting his stance accordingly, Dave lays solid metal on his ball, but it spins left as well, finding the woods just short of where Rob's entered.

Trying to imagine any scenario other than going into the woods, I turn my body so far to the right I'm virtually standing with my back to the trees. I settle into address, visualize and pound down at the ball. It flares out toward the fairway, tries valiantly to carve a straight plot for a second or two, then starts to turn (*Nooooo!* I hear in my mind), and, as though apologizing for an attraction it can't control, turns hard left, flying deep into the woods.

Andrew, the lone rightie among us, uses his slice to the opposite advantage, at first teasing the woods with his ball and then fading it safely onto the fairway. Rob, Dave and I, all now lying two, take our drops and collectively resolve not to waste any more shots. But before trying to make good on this promise, we all notice something at the same time: from here to the green, the canal converges from *both* sides, which would seem physically impossible yet remains as clear as the growing numbers on our scorecards. It is as though we are in one of those movies where the hero, minutes from saving the perfect-looking heroine, is lured into an unfamiliar room where he becomes deeply irked to find that spiked walls are beginning to close in on him.

In case the spiked-walls perception isn't enough, we must now negotiate our way past a dogleg left whose degree of bend we can't discern. The course guide advises us that a good drive into the middle of the fairway will position us well for a solid fade around the dogleg. Consigned as we are to the drop zone beside the woods, this is as relevant for me, Rob and Dave as if the guide had advised that flapping our arms will enable us to fly.

Rattled by the combined effect of the converging waterway and the blind dogleg, Rob tries to cut the corner too tightly, lets his club face open and blasts into the woods for the second shot in a row. After a long laugh, Dave does the same, and his expression changes from one of amusement to one of disbelief.

I stand over my ball, thinking I'd rather be anywhere else in the universe at this moment. Like I did off the tee, I angle my stance, at least at first, far to the right. But my brain pushes hard for me to be a man. *So what if they went in?* it taunts. *You're going to respond by facing away from the dogleg like a scared mouse? Grow a set and take your shot. If it works, you grab two strokes on both of them.*

Swayed by this last point, I angle myself back toward the dog-leg, take my best swing and watch the ball take flight directly into the woods. I feel like bashing my own brain in as punishment, but I try to remember that it's useful for a number of pursuits not related to golf.

Andrew, playing it safe again, punches his second shot forward a fair distance, leaving me, Rob and Dave to somehow process the fact that, after six collective shots, we're carding 12 collective strokes. Each of us hits a decent mid-iron to reach the green in five, then each of us three-putts, making three snow-men. Andrew, having skittled along the right side of the fairway to reach the bunker in front of the green in three, splashes out and two-putts for as easy a skin as he's ever won.

"Good hole, boys," he says.

"You, too," I reply. "Oh, and stick it where the sun don't shine."

For the next few holes I play semi-conservatively, pulling off two bogeys and a double, though no ESPN reporters arrive to cover this feat. At the Old Canal's sixth we climb toward a stunning green perched above the booming water and old walls of the early canal locks.

At 540 yards, six is a brute, but I'm feeling good now that the burger I ate more than an hour ago seems digested. I whack my best drive of the day into the center of the fairway, then follow it with a satisfyingly solid 5-wood that travels straight, if not too far.

With 190 yards still remaining to the green, I'm faced with a decision. After my pitching wedge, my 3-iron is the most unreliable club I own, resulting more often in large ovals of grass sticking to the club than balls soaring into the air. But the chances of my hitting two solid 5-woods in a row seem so remote that I feel foolish for even considering the possibility.

Figuring even a poor 5-wood will get me closer to the green than a potentially thunked 3-iron, I stand over the ball and concentrate. I take my rip. The ball flies off in search of the green. It squeezes every bit of air it can out of its flight, straining, soaring, then, in a moment that changes the single thought held in my brain from *On in three!* to *Why does God hate me?*, lands in one of the three bunkers fronting the elevated green.

I give myself the pep talk every golfer gives himself when standing in a bunker less than 20 feet from the green. *Okay, you may not be on in three, but you're virtually on. Punch this out and roll it toward the hole, two-putt and you still come away with bogey. Simple.*

The three bunkers form a V below the green. The bunker I'm standing in is the point at the base. Scared to sail one past the green, I let my wrists go loose and dink the ball five yards ahead and left, into the bunker forming the left-hand side of the V.

Okay, I tell myself. *That was a lapse. Just a break in concentration. This time, keep the forearm stiff, get it up and on, then two-putt and you save double.*

Committed to keeping my forearm stiff, I swing solidly. My ball shoots off the front lip and ricochets up, right and into the third of the three bunkers. With three consecutive shots, I've found three different bunkers separated by a total of no more than 30 feet.

By the end of the two nine-hole rounds, Andrew, having flown under the radar of our lefty-dominated slapstick all day, comes away victorious, with 95. Rob, Dave and I, all comfortably above the century line, tip our hats and tell him we hope he gets hit by a truck on the way home.

As we drop off our carts and walk back toward the clubhouse, I think one last time about the gargantuan processes that have jostled together to continually reconfigure this landscape. In the distance, I think I hear the low roar of the Falls, although it could be in my mind.

"Round's over," Dave says. "You can't get any of those shots back." He hands me an orange Gatorade and smiles.

The Perfectionist

As I dial the number in Colorado, I feel my breath catch. It's like I'm in high school again, calling the girl I like for a date but then, with each ring, feeling my brain transform into a block of ice.

The physical sensation is the same as it was then, and so is the question growing louder in my head: *What am I going to talk about?*

Just as I'd script the opening of those high school calls, I've jotted two pages' worth of questions for this. But I'm looking over the questions as the phone keeps ringing, and they look ridiculous. Who am I to think I can shoot the breeze with this guy? He's one of the best golfers in history. My last two rounds were 106 and 110, and for me that was pretty good.

Ask me to trade barbs with other writers and I'll snap into form faster than Voltaire at a party. Request a profile on John Grisham or J.K. Rowling and I'll not only track them down but also guarantee to get them chatting inside three minutes. I can talk about the things they can—about the things they love.

I can discuss the finer points of hyphenation or debate proper semicolon use until the cows come home. But how in the name of Old Tom Morris am I supposed to engage a guy who's won a major championship and captained a Ryder Cup team? Should I warm him up with the story of the time I short-hopped the flagstick on that 86-yard par 3 when I was 15? Or maybe I could talk about the changes to the game over the past 50 years, the problem being that I've been alive for only 33 of them. Maybe he'll be riveted by the story about my friend Keith hitting the gazebo at Rolling Hills that time and it caroming off and hitting him right in the—

"Hello?"

I'm frozen. The voice on the other end belongs to Dow Finsterwald Sr., the guy who took home the 1958 PGA Championship, the guy who took Palmer and Player to a playoff at Augusta in '62. I might as well call Gary Kasparov to talk about my castling technique.

Dow sounds mild and welcoming, throwing me off even more. I can't remember the approach I'd planned. All I remember is what I wanted to avoid. Don't ask about the win in '58 too early, as though it's the only highlight in a career that included 11 tour victories. Don't bore him with method questions he's heard a thousand times. Don't let the interview turn into a discussion about the swashbuckling Arnie, who happened to come on the scene around the same time as Dow.

Trying to ignore my feelings of fraudulence, presumption and gastrointestinal unease, I spend a couple of minutes refreshing Dow on the purpose of my book, all the while trying to collect myself and determine which one or two of the 30 questions I wrote down might be worthy of asking. He tries to help me along as

I cover a few mindless topics, my questions coming off like my golf swing—awkward, confused and completely lacking rhythm or pace.

Out of panic, I ask him what I'd considered a throwaway question, scrawled in the margins: "What do you think about when you're standing over a golf ball?" I'd actually like to know the answer to this, but I assumed it might sound cutesy, or just plain dumb, so I'd asterisked it as a last-resort option. As a general rule, one shouldn't have to use last-resort questions in the first five minutes of an interview.

"Well, it's something different every day," says Dow, his voice perking up. "Today it was the amount of pressure being exerted by the middle two fingers of my right hand. That thought might last a couple of days before I start getting focused on something else. One day I might be thinking about balance and trying to keep my weight from getting out on my toes. Another day it might be about keeping the left arm a little firmer, since I have a tendency to break down. The day after that, something new. Then it might go back and start all over again."

Inadvertently, I've hit a nerve. I ask him how many swing thoughts he tries to focus on at a time.

"Generally, one. It should be mostly reflex once you get over the ball. Ninety percent of your mental bit is done prior to address: where you want to go or don't want to go, your yardage, swing mechanics. You put all that in your little computer up there, then step up and hit. Take Jack, probably the greatest player ever—he had a tendency to stand over the ball a long time. Cary Middle-coff, who won three majors, stood over it a long time, too, but he did a lot of bouncing of the club. Hogan got to the point where he stayed over his putter a long time."

Prior to the call, I reminded myself a dozen times not to become mesmerized by the names. But I'm undeniably starstruck. When Dow tells me Hogan stood over his putts, he isn't guessing or relaying third-party information; he's telling me because he stood on greens with Hogan.

Realizing I've been pausing a few seconds too long, I ask another random question from the margins of my notes: "What's your favorite club?"

"Oh, I guess I've been decent with my putter over the years," Dow says. I think I hear him enjoying the question. "I've never been one of those players who changes putters every month, or who goes to the course with three different ones and sees which one feels best when he gets there, or who uses a heavier putter on slower greens. I've always believed in the idea that it's easier to get used to one club and adjust speed according to what changes. Your body isn't constant. The greens aren't constant. But the weight and feel of a single putter is constant, so you can at least keep that within your control. That's the reason I used the same wooden-shaft putter from '55 to '63."

He's talking the way I might about the rules of grammar—expansively, obsessively, even a bit obliviously. And I love it.

Thinking we've established a nice tempo, I revert to safe questions. I ask if he comes from a golfing family. No. I ask him whether he recalls picking up a golf club for the first time. Not really. I ask if his son, Dow Jr., is a similar type of golfer. Shorter swing, he says. Much better left arm. Longer than he ever was.

He says these things with passing interest, as though we were walking down an interesting path together and I've now guided him back onto the same road he's walked dozens of times. I'm too flustered to ask about the '58 win or the '62 playoff. Did you know, I ask him, that *Asian Golf Monthly* recently ranked you sixty-third on the all-time list of golfers?

"Well, I think that's pretty generous," Dow chuckles. "But I don't lose sleep over those kinds of things."

He pauses, but I try to resist pouncing. Through the silence I believe I can hear him preparing to say more.

"I'd probably put Jack at the top," he says, answering a question I haven't asked. "All things being equal, it would be pretty hard to pick between him and Tiger, who certainly does some marvelous things. A lot of guys would be right there in the argument if circumstances were the same. If you had Jones and Hogan and Snead in their prime, put them in a time capsule and put them all together with Tiger, it would be hard to name just one. These guys had something inside."

An interviewer need do only two things well: ask good questions, then get out of the way. "What did they have inside?" I ask. Then I shut up.

"They had a mental toughness. I don't think there's any question the mental aspect of golf is tremendous. I attribute it to the amount of time you have between shots. Walking 250 yards to your ball, there's a lot of time to think. It hurts some players because they don't have that mental makeup. Those who excel are able to keep their minds on track. There are exceptions, of course. Jimmy Demaret was a wonderful player, and he talked to the gallery constantly."

At the casual mention of yet another towering golf figure, I again become rapt. I'd forgotten for a moment that, when Dow mentions Jones and Hogan and Snead, he's mentioning them as naturally as I might mention Rob, Dave and Andrew. These were his peers.

I don't know if I've asked another question, but Dow has moved on. He's talking about his own commitment to gaining a psychological edge. "My father taught me the importance of practice, which I took to heart. There was a picture of Hogan I always kept, containing the quote *If you can't outplay them, outwork them.* I hit a whole lot of golf balls. I can remember many nights saying to my caddy, as it got darker and darker, 'One more bag. Let's do one more.'"

I can feel myself itching to ask about '58. But it isn't yet time. I want to know how he got into the game in the first place. Did he trip on a golf club one day and fall in love with the shape and feel of it? Did he see the game as a sunbathed path to fame and riches? Did he want to become great at something to impress some girl?

"In '44," he begins, "the pro at the local nine-hole course in my hometown of Athens, Ohio, was called into service. They needed someone to sweep the locker room and take care of things. My dad told me that if I took the job, I might be able to save enough money to go to the World Series."

Though I'm delighted to discover that this golf legend first started playing because of his love for baseball, I try not to act too excited. Instead I ask him what it was like to be at the Series, while hearing in my mind, *1944—Browns vs. Cardinals. The St. Louis Showdown. Cards' victory. Second title in three years.*

"Oh, I didn't go," he says.

"You hadn't saved enough?"

"I'd saved enough."

"Then what did you do with the money?"

"Bought a set of clubs."

Now we're both feeling it. There's momentum. We ping-pong enjoyably among several topics: how he suggested to Hale Irwin's university football coach that Hale might have the tools to be a great golfer; his initial opposition to allowing Europeans in the Ryder Cup ("Just one more time I've been wrong," says Dow); his experience captaining the Ryder squad in '77 ("I told each player, 'If you usually drink a quart of whiskey the night before a tournament, do it here, too'"); his continuing search for the perfect swing ("I still devote quite a bit of time to tinkering with this or that club. A golf game is a fleeting thing.")

Then it's time—or at least I can no longer wait. I apologize to Dow for having to ask so obvious a question, but ask it I must. Few people on the planet can say they've won a major on the PGA Tour. I don't want to machine-gun you with an endless series of questions about the '58 PGA victory, I say, so instead I'll ask a single three-parter. How did you feel going in? When did you know the tournament was yours? And does it seem like yesterday, a distant memory or somewhere in between?

"I always thought the same thing before each tournament: I'm going to play as well as I can, and what happens, happens. Arnold had won the Masters, so he was obviously on my mind. Casper was playing well. And it was Littler's first PGA, I think. I was very nicely asked to come back to Llanerch for the fortieth anniversary of that win a few years ago, and, as I stood on the course, some of the shots came back pretty vividly. There was a par 3—I want to say it was the thirteenth, or maybe the twelfth, about 165 yards. I played a poor shot off the tee. I was playing with Snead, who'd been leading going into the last day."

I was playing with Snead. A chill runs up my spine.

"He put it on the green. With my second shot, I hit some kind of wedge over a tree, stuck it ten feet from the hole and sank the putt. Snead three-putted. That was big. Going into the last three holes, I had a two-shot lead. On each of those holes, I made putts that ended up two or two-and-a-half feet past the hole. People were surprised, because I'd been dubbed a very conservative player, and they thought I'd suddenly turned aggressive. Actually, I was only playing percentages, making sure each time that, if I missed, my next putt would be uphill."

Sure, I'd like to say I often use that very same strategy. Then again, I'd also like to say I'm dating the Dallas Cowboys Cheerleaders. I say nothing.

"When I got it on the green at 18, I had three putts to win. I only had one thought: just don't step on your pick. I two-putted, and it was mine."

Soon the energy shifts again, as though revisiting the win has drained Dow, and I begin to sense I've taken up enough of the man's time. Before letting him go, I ask whether he has time for three more questions. First, I want to know how he feels about his reputation as a perfectionist from tee to green.

"Oh, I've missed a lot of greens and fairways," he says, before allowing his armor of modesty to crack ever so slightly. "But I seem to have missed mostly on the side where recovery was possible. I had a knack for curving the ball. If the pin were on the right side, I'd aim left-center and hope to work it back to the flag." Realizing he's just admitted he's a better-than-average golfer, he issues an immediate qualifier. "Of course, in those days you could hook and slice more easily when it served your purposes. Balls today, with the different-sized dimples and patterns, tend to straighten out. So I had an advantage."

Next, I want tips. I tell Dow my game is certifiably lousy. Without seeing me play (and trust me, I tell him, you do not want to see me play), give me your top three pieces of advice.

"One, have a reasonably good grip. There isn't only one way to do it, but however you do it, do it consistently. Two, strive for balance. So much of it is balance. Three, keep your head steady. It doesn't have to be rigid, but it does have to be pretty still. I've always felt the natural point for the head to start moving is when the trailing shoulder gets to the chin, at which point the club head is probably two to three feet off the ground in front of where the ball was."

Just the view I've always maintained. It's like we're golf soulmates. Last question: "Do you feel the game has changed from 50 years ago?"

"The game is the game," he says. "What I find astounding is the size and strength of today's golfers. Back then, the average guy was maybe five-ten. Nelson might have been six feet, but that was uncommon. Today, the guys doing well are big fellows, six feet and one-ninety, that kind of thing."

He pauses. I have the choice either to wait, hoping he has more to say, or to shoehorn one last question in. I wait.

"One interesting thing is how all the guys who have played hockey hit the ball with exceptional distance, whether they're big or not. Weir, for instance—little guy, but he can really smack it. But I guess being a Canuck, you'd know that, *eh*?" Dow chuckles. The joke pleases me. As a rule, when any interview subject feels comfortable enough to take a shot at me involving maple syrup, igloos, beer, hockey or the word "eh," they're happy with the way things have gone.

I have a theory, I tell Dow. Hockey players, to succeed, must master the same physical concept as golfers. A puck picked cleanly off the ice will only slide weakly along it, but when the stick coming at it trampolines off the ice a fraction of an inch behind, the puck becomes a missile. When those with hockey in their blood address a golf ball, they understand this and intuitively hit it the right way, driving the ball into, and off of, the ground instead of trying to scoop it into the air.

"I never considered that," says Dow. "But you're probably right. Thank you."

The perfectionist has just thanked me for my golf insight. He's made me feel smart about the game.

He's even better than I thought.

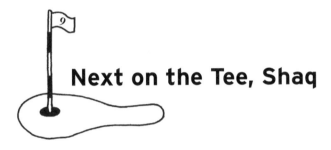

Next on the Tee, Shaq

It's time we admitted the truth: today's golfers have become so good that they're beginning to lose our attention. Sure, it's fun to witness Tiger make a golf ball do things that would have gotten him burned at the stake a few centuries ago, or to see Annika flex muscles that cause her playing partners to blanch with fear—but, like boyfriends or girlfriends whose moves were thrilling at first, these players no longer surprise us. We recognize that they're wonderful at what they do, but we also know what to expect. For the good of the game, something must be done.

Two potential solutions come to mind. The first is to ban from the tour every player who has finished in the top three in any tournament over the past five years. Removing enough of these elite players would ensure a more erratic, and therefore more engaging, level of play.

This option, of course, is unfair to those who have practised so many years for the opportunity to one day don an unattractive green jacket. Nonetheless, it is fun to imagine what some of our more celebrated players might be doing if not golfing. Ernie Els might open a stress-reduction clinic. Sergio Garcia would head up a psychology lab specializing in obsessive-compulsive disorders, with a sub-specialization in the rare condition IRE, or Incessant Regripping Syndrome. And Tiger Woods would become a world-famous illusionist headlining his own show in Las Vegas. If he can perform the feats he does on a golf course, imagine what he could do with state-of-the-art pyrotechnics and topless dancers.

The second, more appropriate, solution demands that we confess another truth. There's a part of each of us that prefers watching the celebrity tournaments, the ones in which professionals from other sports nub their drives 30 feet, movie actors try to overcome their lack of ability with charming wit and perfect skin and American presidents come close to decapitating innocent spectators. These events are truly enthralling because they involve more than simple club selection or waiting to see who hits water going for the island green on the second-to-last hole. When club meets ball in these events, anything can happen, and that makes for great golf.

Given this reality, I suggest a new rule for the PGA tour. Every tournament should include at least one non-tour foursome for the purpose of balancing out the professionals whose brilliance has come to bore us. In case this new rule is adopted (and I don't see any reason it wouldn't be, unless you count the fact that the PGA has never acknowledged one of my suggestions before), I offer some possible foursomes that would be sure to make the average tournament more enjoyable:

Sean Connery, Roger Moore, Timothy Dalton, Pierce Brosnan

Never mind all those debates about who has the most charisma, the most powerful screen presence or the best hairline. How do you determine the best Bond? I'll tell you how. Who can get up and down from the sand with the round hanging in the balance? (Incidentally, why haven't any Bond films started with 007 needing to sink an eight-foot putt to prevent some evil megalomaniac from achieving world domination? That's more than suspense; it's outright terror.)

Tony Blair, George W. Bush, Vladimir Putin, Jacques Chirac

World leaders never get anything done by holding summits or conferences. Instead they sit around for days and then announce they haven't a clue how to solve the world's problems, though they at least agree on that fact. Apart from sitting in a classroom or one's spouse requesting a household chore, nothing clears the mind like a round of golf. Get these men out on the links for an afternoon and watch the resolutions fall like dominos. *It's such an exquisite day, and I'm only three over for the round. Let's disarm after all.*

Maya Angelou, Nelson Mandela, Tenzin Gyatso (the Dalai Lama), Uncle Ted

Each of these individuals is known for his or her inner tranquility, outward calm or overall equanimity. (You'll have to take my word for it regarding Uncle Ted. You could light this guy's shoes on fire and he'd say, "Would someone mind dousing my loafers? My feet are getting quite toasty.") Let's give these unflappable souls a downhill lie to a protected green and see how long they remain at peace with the universe. It's not that I have a twisted desire to transform those naturally composed into loons, but you have to admit it would be fun to see the Dalai Lama holler a string of curses and send a driver twirling down the fairway.

NAOMI CAMPBELL, COURTNEY LOVE, SEAN PENN, MIKE TYSON

In contrast to the previous group, the reputations of this foursome are based not on composure but on habitual crankiness. I'd mostly like to watch these powder kegs play a round to see who would snap first. I'd also be curious to find out which of them could toss a club the farthest. (Side bet for this group: Who would have the most clubs still intact in his or her bag upon returning to the clubhouse?)

BILLY JOEL, SHERYL CROW, ELTON JOHN, NORAH JONES

When was the last time you heard a decent tune about the grand old game? Get these songsters out playing 18 and they might be inspired to put aside the tired themes we always hear (I lost my girl and want her back; never give up on your dreams; down with the establishment) to instead dedicate time to a much more important subject: golf. It's a topic so rich in material that the songs would virtually write themselves. *Look at me with pity, brother/ Seems the bunker's snared another/Flight path looks just like the Seine/ Put me down for six again.*

BRAD PITT, JUDE LAW, ELIZABETH HURLEY, GISELE BUNDCHEN

On those rare days when the pros aren't playing up to their usual level, we fans need something more exciting than the leader laying up at 18 to keep us absorbed. This foursome could spray balls all over the course for 72 holes and we'd barely notice.

SHAQUILLE O'NEAL, DAVID BECKHAM, EDGERRIN JAMES, ICHIRO SUZUKI

Each of these athletes dominates his sport differently—O'Neal by exploiting agility that no 300-pound seven-footer should possess, Beckham by eliciting unnatural acts from a soccer ball, James by finding inventive ways to slice through a line of helmeted ogres, and Ichiro by wielding a baseball bat like a magic wand. But golf is unique in its capacity to render natural physical gifts extraneous. Put a putter in Shaq's hands and see if he isn't begging to return to the hardwood faster than you can say "undulating green."

ANNA KOURNIKOVA, DOLPH LUNDGREN, EDDIE "THE EAGLE" EDWARDS, SAMANTHA FOX

Since these individuals were obviously misguided in their original pursuits (and if you don't believe that, rent *Red Scorpion*), it might make sense for them to find out whether golf is their actual calling. Besides, imagine how entertained we'd be while they try.

JOHN UPDIKE, STEPHEN KING, TONI MORRISON, MARGARET ATWOOD

Players deft of tongue, whether or not deft of club, would vastly improve the game, particularly after really awful shots. I'd continue watching even after a match was effectively over if I knew there was the possibility of someone declaring, "I struck that ball with all the precise fury of a panther on the hunt. My club came slashing down silently through the summer air, the powder-blue sky its backdrop, and met the ball square at its face, promising good fortune. My front arm was as stiff as a private at attention, my hip turn as smooth as a wave curling into shore. But the ball, my friend, had other ideas; the ball knew its destiny." At least it's better than, "Christ, another one in the drink."

SIEGFRIED & ROY, DAVID COPPERFIELD, DAVID BLAINE

The best golfers are, in essence, magicians, since they have learned to persuade little white balls to do things alien to the rest of us. The players in this foursome are known for making objects vanish before our eyes, performing card tricks that boggle the mind and convincing exotic tigers to play nice (most of the time). But can they hit a lob wedge?

CHRIS ROCK, HUGH GRANT, JERRY SEINFELD, JIM CARREY

The best way to keep sane during any golf round is by laughing, particularly at your playing partners. When Andrew shanks his 3-wood for the fourth time in a round and all I can come up with is, "Maybe it's time to retire that club, pal," I wish I could inhabit the brain of one of these men, even for a moment. That way, even if I weren't impressing anyone with my stroke, I could at least break them up with zingers all day. After missing yet another fairway, I'd finally be able to offer something more clever than, "Well, it's been a pleasure. I'm off to slit my wrists." Just picturing Hugh Grant missing a three-footer and saying "Ah, excellent" gives me a chuckle.

Arnold Schwarzenegger, Sylvester Stallone, Jean-Claude Van Damme, Jackie Chan

These guys have been paid zillions to pretend they can maneuver stealth bombers, outrun machine-gun spray, paralyze evil geniuses with a subtle pinch to the neck or diffuse intricate bombs in less time than it takes to eat a handful of popcorn. It's not that I begrudge their success; it's just that I think a dogleg or two helps gain a little perspective.

Scoring with the Ladies

Returning to one's childhood home is forever strange. Every-thing feels comfortable and familiar, yet oddly foreign. You can't tell if everything is smaller or if you're just looking at it through different eyes. Every step is a memory, every corner a reminder.

Driving north through Thornhill, the Toronto suburb where I spent the first 24 years of my life, I see ghosts everywhere. Through the windows of the greasy spoon Golden Star, my friend Ernie and I are exploring the mysteries of our teenage existence while downing cheeseburgers and plates of onion rings. Outside the doors of the hockey arena is my ten-year-old self awkwardly carrying a large duffel bag, my father toting my sticks beside me. Within the walls of the library I'm sitting at a table, my eyes rivet-ed to an H.G. Wells story, a voice inside telling me it knows what it wants to do in life. There's the schoolyard where I opened my heart to Heidi Turner; the track where I ran hundred-meter sprints at dawn; the park where I sat and wrote dozens of bad poems at a single sitting.

The appearance of a new element surprises me. Barely poking out of the trees at the bottom of the hill on Yonge Street is a wooden sign with the words *Ladies' Golf Club of Toronto* carved into it. Above the words is a picture of a woman in a long skirt swinging an old-fashioned golf club. Her swing looks good.

Curious, I turn into the tree-lined driveway and follow it past a stone-encircled fountain to the clubhouse, a white, shuttered building that looks like it could have been transplanted from a beachfront in Massachusetts. When I get out of the car, a number of women in shorts and tailored golf tops turn toward me. I feel like a spy who has parachuted into enemy territory.

When I enter the pro shop, it's as though a Martian has walked through the doors. The two women behind the desk regard me oddly, as though, in reading *Ladies' Golf Club of Toronto*, I've somehow misinterpreted the word *Ladies*.

"Hi," I say, pulling out my business card. "My name is I.J. Schecter. I'm a golf writer. Is this a new club?"

"The Ladies' was built in 1924," says one of the ladies.

"Ah. Yes, right. You know, it's funny, I actually grew up around here but was never aware of it."

The fact that my card is still dangling from my fingers tells me they're less than impressed. One of them tries to push up a polite smile. The other looks at me as though I'm a cardboard cutout.

"I'm in the middle of writing a golf book, and I'd love to write about your club. Do you think I might be able to talk to the manager, or maybe even get to play a round with some of your members?"

"Oh, I don't think so," says the one with the quarter-smile.

Potential interviewees rarely say yes the first time. Eventually they're happy to talk, but their first reaction is almost always a reflexive no. I don't flinch. Turning these no's into yes's is one of my specialties.

At the moment, there is only one issue. Usually, before I even approach, I've done so much homework I can predict what color underwear my subject is wearing. I have to improvise, but that's okay. If you want to get information, you have to learn to think on your feet. It's all about winning people over, something I have a knack for.

"It's a club for women, then?"

They look at each other. Quarter Smile says, "Yes, Ladies' is a club for women."

"And the membership is up to, what …"

"Several hundred. Excuse me, but we're very busy." She clicks the top off a yellow Hi-Liter and turns her attention to the tee-time sheet on the desk. The other woman turns to adjust a display of golf balls.

"I understand. Well, thanks for your time. I'll just leave my card. Perhaps someone could give me a call." Quarter Smile looks at me like I must be deaf, not realizing I'm actually just stubborn.

I continue through Thornhill, every street, store and sidewalk mapping onto a different part of my memory. How did I not know of the existence of a golf club open since 1924? The answer is obvious enough. It's a ladies' golf club. I'm not a lady, and growing up I wasn't a golfer. Okay, I'm still not a golfer, but I do play golf.

Once home, I visit the club's website. I discover that The Ladies' maintains unique standing in the golf universe. The LGCT is the only remaining club in North America founded by women for women. In other words, no boys allowed back in 1924 when it was founded, and no boys allowed today.

It wasn't easy forming such a club. Men in 1924 weren't exactly fighting for the opportunity to champion women's athletics, and fewer yet were willing to fork over thousands of dollars in support of a club whose mandate would be to exclude men.

That's where Ada Mackenzie came in. A magnificent golfer and indomitable spirit, Ada had made her mark in tournaments in Canada, the U.S. and Britain. It was during her visits to the latter that she learned of clubs that had formed specifically for women. A lightbulb went on. Despite being able to hit a golf ball better than most men, Ada had spent a good deal of her time just trying to find times and places to play, or even to practicse. Most golf clubs were owned by men, and most men had little concern over the desire of women to enjoy, or, dare they think it, master the game.

As I read further about Ada, the piece I plan to include in the book starts to materialize. I wonder if I can track down someone who knew her. Doubtful, since that would make my potential interview subject over a hundred years old, and hundred-year-old interviewees rarely give good sound bytes. Maybe I could find one of her descendants. I make a note on a Post-it and stick it onto my laptop.

I learn that the site of the current LGCT was originally a farm estate accessible only by rail car. The estate was owned by a gent with the marvelous name of Strafford Watson. Ada had approached Mr. Watson informing him that she was interested in using his land for a ladies' golf club. Mr. Watson had told her this wasn't a problem, provided she could raise the eighty-five thousand dollars he was willing to sell it for.

I think of starting the piece with Ada peering toward the property, imagining groups of women enjoying one another's company and hitting golf balls down beautifully manicured fairways. I wonder if I could locate a relative of Strafford Watson. I'm really looking forward to writing this piece.

Unwilling to accept no for an answer, Ada obtained support from several prominent women, and a few men, in the area, who collectively purchased 30 bonds for a thousand dollars each. With the purchase came the condition that Ada must secure 300 memberships for her club, at a hundred dollars each, by the time the sale of the estate closed.

Ada had done her best, but it looked like her best wouldn't be enough. Two hours before the deadline, she was still eight thousand dollars short of Strafford Watson's asking price.

It turned out Ada wasn't done by a long shot. She somehow contrived a meeting with J.P. Bickell, in line to become president of the Toronto Maple Leafs. There was one snag. A sports enthusiast he was; a women's sports enthusiast he wasn't. In fact, he had a pretty low opinion of women overall. Though he accepted the meeting, he insisted it be conducted on his verandah so Ada wouldn't have to come inside.

Nice guy, I think to myself. Good luck getting the money, Ada.

But Ada is more resourceful than I know. She somehow comes away with the eight thousand, gets to the esteemed Strafford Watson in time, and suddenly brings her dream into the world of reality.

I nod emphatically. *Attagirl, Ada. Knew you could do it.*

I check out the other tabs on the LGCT website, looking for a contact name. I've gone in through the back door plenty of times. All it takes is getting to one person.

I find a name listed under General Club Operations. That's close enough. It's a man's name, which is good. He's my ticket behind the walls of the fortress.

Clicking on his name takes me to a generic e-mail window. I'm not a fan of general mailboxes—one usually has a better chance of receiving a reply from the Pope—so I close the window, noting the address on a Post-it just in case.

Instead, I call. While the phone rings on the other end, I get to wondering who I'll be paired with when I play the course. Sweet, older, slow-swinging women who talk endlessly about their grandchildren? Power moms with golf-lesson swings and gym-toned arms? Teenage girls trying to become the next Michelle Wie?

I reach his voicemail. I leave a standard professional-but-friendly message, making sure to casually note my credentials and drop a few important magazine names, which will intrigue him enough to call back. I hang up expecting a return call within 48 hours.

Three days pass. I go back to the website and decide to send an inquiry using the generic e-mail, which I'll follow up with another phone call in a few days. Must be a busy place. This time I emphasize my credits a little more, since I want to make sure I get them curious. Every golf course on the planet likes publicity. They'll call.

In the meantime, I study my subject more, reading through some of the other website tabs. Mostly I discover this is a club that takes itself seriously. The guidelines page informs me that shorts or skirts must be no shorter than five inches above the top of the knee when standing. Also, that pull-on drawstring shorts/slacks, athletic shorts and/or bike shorts are not permitted. And finally, that no jeans, jean-style pants or denim apparel of any color is permitted. These rules are much more elaborate than the general principle governing most private men's clubs: Try not to act like an ass.

The LGCT, it seems, is sticky about the appearance of its members from head to toe. Its guidelines for socks reads

Sport specific socks are permitted as follows:
Sockette: a footie with a cushioned sole that reaches to the ankle
Quarter: a medium-weight athletic sock that reaches just above the
*   anklebone, often with cuffs*
Crew: a medium-weight calf-length sock
Knee: socks reaching just below the knee—no stripes

Below the socks guidelines is a note indicating that golf club logos are acceptable, but company logos that may or may not be golf related will be accepted "as long as they do not overwhelm the garment."

I sympathize with any LGCT member trying to figure out if her clothes fall within the guidelines, but this is good material. I scrawl a note on a Post-it to remind myself to record the heights of my playing partners' socks when I meet them. That's gold. The piece is feeling like 3,000 words, give or take. Before shutting down the computer, I notice the LGCT even has a quaint mission statement: To provide a place for women, desirous of a private club atmosphere, to play golf. Am I glad I found this place. It's going to be one of the standout pieces in the book.

The next morning, I boot up my laptop and smile when a message from the LGCT appears in my Inbox. I click on it, wondering whether I should play the course on a weekday afternoon or weekend morning.

"Dear Mr. Schecter," it reads, "Thank you for your inquiry regarding Ladies' Golf Club of Toronto. We are not interested in coverage at this time."

I read the e-mail a second time, trying to find the part where it offers me a complimentary round and asks for more information about my book. Curiously, that section is missing.

I dial the General Club Operations guy again. This time, he answers. "Good morning," I say. "It's I.J. Schecter calling—I left you a message last week about potentially including Ladies' in my upcoming golf book, and I'm just following up."

"I'm sorry, what did you say your name was?"

"I.J. Schecter."

"Oh, yes," he says. "You called before, didn't you?"

"That's right. I'm writing a book on golf, which will include coverage of a number of different courses, and I'd really like to—"

"We're not really interested in that sort of thing right now."

"I understand. It's actually kind of a different book, where I won't be just talking about courses in the typical way. Instead I'm planning to—"

"We're just very busy. Perhaps you'd like to call back in a few months."

"I do appreciate what you're saying. The issue is that the book is actually coming out next spring, and so my deadline for finishing it is quite soon."

"I'm sorry. I don't think I can help you."

"I see."

I don't get it. He's a man, shutting out another man from getting even a peek into the sanctuary. What goes on there? What do they do? What secrets do they have? And why won't they let me be a part of it?

I notice a tab on the website called Employment Opportunities. Maybe I'll fake my way in by applying for a job. I click on the tab. "Throughout the year," it says, "there are periodic openings in the dining section and other areas of the club. You may check here for openings throughout the year. Ladies' Golf Club of Toronto is an equal-opportunity employer." I'll just bet they are. I click on Current Openings, where I'm informed that Ladies' has completed its hiring for 2005; however, opportunities may arise during the season, and, if I'm hard-working, high-energy and customer-focused, I should feel free to get in touch.

I send in a resumé and cover letter indicating my connection to Thornhill and my eagerness to work at a private golf club. My follow-up call two days later is directed to the woman in charge of hiring.

"Hi, I sent in a resumé earlier this week," I say. "I'd like to confirm you received it."

"I'm sure we've received it. Thank you."

"Would it be possible to make certain? I'm heading out of town for a few days and just wanted to make sure it went through in case anyone should call while I'm away."

"We're not looking to do any further hiring this year, so it's unlikely anyone will be calling. We thank you for your interest."

"Oh. Okay. Um, thank you."

They're playing hardball. No problem. I've gotten around bigger roadblocks before. In the end, they'll be thrilled for the exposure.

I decide to do some on-site reconnaissance work. Okay, not quite on-site. More like underground, covert ops kind of work. I drive to the course again, this time with a plan. I almost always have a plan. My plan is to park at the far edge of the lot and stand behind my car. When I see a pair or trio of club members walking toward their cars, I will pretend I happen to be walking from my car toward the clubhouse. I will say, "Excuse me, ladies. I'm researching a piece on your club here for a book. I assume you're members?" They'll nod. I'll initiate a casual dialogue about the club. They won't know I'm actually embedding several questions designed to unearth critical information. After gaining their trust over a minute or two, I'll start asking more direct questions. Are they aware of the club's heritage and the story of Ada Mackenzie? What does she mean to them today? What do they love about hitting a good golf shot?

As I continue to brainstorm in the car, I get excited about the piece again. So unique a piece, and so rich. I bet I'll get answers that offer a funny contrast to men's. Men want to murder the ball, women like the soft feeling of a graceful swing—that kind of thing. I won't lead the questions in that direction, but if I get those kinds of answers, great. Okay, maybe I'll lead them a bit. I'll ask them their opinions on the Hootie Johnson–Martha Burk controversy of a few years ago, then whether they agree that women shouldn't play at men's clubs just as men shouldn't play at theirs.

I park and wait. After a few minutes, two middle-aged women in shorts and vests come out chatting. I emerge in mid-stride, angle my walk toward them and say, "Excuse me, ladies. I'm researching a piece on your club here for a book. I assume you're members?"

"I'm sorry, we're in a hurry," one of them says, and they scoot to their cars.

I try again a few minutes later, this time with a woman by herself wheeling her clubs along in a pull-cart. "Excuse me, ma'am, I'm researching a book—"

"I'm afraid I can't talk," she says. In a flash, she's into her car and out of the parking lot. What am I, the bogeyman? What do they do to men in this place? Do they take them out back to tar-and-feather them? Do they tease them about the way they over-accessorize as compensation for not being secure enough in their manhood? Do they grind them up and use them for turf?

After half a dozen attempts to strike up conversations and the same number of outright rejections, I feel more frustrated than a freshman at a school dance. This is good, though. Good challenge. It's going to take all my wits. It's time to break out the heavy ammunition. Time to write a letter.

I go home, close the door to my office and begin to compose. Holding to my belief in fraternity, I address it to the General Club Operations guy. I draft a few different structures and play with each one until the strongest makes itself obvious. I work and rework every paragraph until the raw structure is intact. Then I massage and refine, ruthlessly attacking each sentence, challenging every word to prove it belongs. I make tiny adjustments here and there, small tweaks to this or that. Finally I read it over, then a second time, then a third, and smile. This will do it.

I take Oliver, nearing his first birthday, on a stroller walk to mail the letter. "I'm not sure what the deal is, my man," I say. "It's like a secret society there."

"Aaaahhhhh," he replies.

"Yes, it is weird. But no worries. This is going to get us in." I show him the envelope.

"OwooaaAAAAA!" he says, bouncing up and down and throwing his arms above his head.

When we reach the mailbox I unstrap him, hold him in front of it and let him drop the letter in. "Good man," I say.

"Da-DA," he says, pinching my nose.

"You got that right, mister," I say. "They'll be putty in daddy's hands now."

A week later, neither I nor Oliver has received word from Ladies', or any of the ladies at Ladies', or any of the men at Ladies'. I call, introduce myself to the receptionist and mention the letter I sent to General Club Operations guy.

"Oh, yes," she says, "he did receive your letter."

"Excellent." Now we're getting somewhere. I wink at Oliver and give him a way-to-go nod. He tosses a ball backwards over his head and cracks up.

"But he asked me to tell you he'd like to pass."

"Sorry?"

"He's not interested in any coverage for the course just now. He asked me to convey that message to you. But he wanted to thank you for the letter. I read it, too. It was very nice."

I hang up, then join Oliver on the floor. He dives onto my lap and laughs in a series of little gasps. Then he grabs two plastic balls and raps them together, looking up at me as though he's just discovered a new branch of scientific investigation.

I decide the LGCT piece doesn't quite fit into the book. Maybe it will work as part of another project down the line. For now, though, I just can't see the value.

Anyway, it's not like I can't take a hint.

Thoughts on a Backswing

Optimal mental readiness, in almost every sport, results from a kind of oxymoronic Zen state—utter focus combined with virtual absence of thought. Almost any professional athlete will tell you the same thing: Thinking, in the end, only interferes with physical effort.

While this sage advice certainly makes all of us feel a lot better about the fact that we probably couldn't hit a three at the buzzer to save the galaxy, there's a crucial element the pros are forgetting. They've spent countless hours building muscle memory that allows them to compute the trajectory of a wicked slider, leave their feet to catch an overthrown pass or hit a clean 3-iron *without having to remind themselves how to do it each time*. Asked to place thought completely aside, we recreational athletes are left with our own version of muscle memory, equivalent to a blank chalkboard.

In golf, thinking is far more hazardous than it is in any other sport. A hitter standing in the batter's box might be considering what to have for dinner and his hands might still do him the favor of swinging at the ball at just the right moment. A running back, finding the pigskin suddenly in his grasp, might have been musing a moment earlier about an attractive girl in the stands, but it's a good bet his legs will still get him the hell out of there on instinct as an alternative to having every one of their bones crushed. But a golfer standing over his ball, if not focused on the task at hand, might stand there for centuries, and no force in the universe is going to lift his club off the ground.

I raise this argument with my friend Todd, a sales executive who, having spent more time wooing clients on the golf course than working in his office over the course of his career, suddenly discovered one day that he had become a tremendous golfer. He responds by telling me to empty my mind, relax and just let the swing come naturally. I tell him my natural swing produces scores that have too many digits. I don't want to let it come naturally; what I want is an artificially produced, expertly manufactured, machine-calibrated swing that allows me to take part in conversations about golf handicaps without always having to make the joke "My handicap is that I suck at golf. Ha, ha. Ahem."

"Okay," he says, "we'll compromise. You can think, but only enough to retain a single swing thought."

I'm suspicious of a guy whose profession involves convincing people to do things they didn't know they wanted to do before talking to him. But I keep listening.

"For instance, today, don't try to work on anything but keeping yourself aligned to the target. Before every shot, remind yourself of that thought one time, then let your mind relax. Don't overthink. Don't even focus on the hole. Just relax. Let your mind run free. Let your natural motion take over. Trust your hands. Trust the swing. Trust that everything will work together in har—"

"Sorry, were you saying something?"

"I was reminding you to—"

"I was just joking! You said let your mind run free, so I was pretending I wasn't listening! Get it?"

"Good one," he says.

"Okay," I reply, resting my driver behind the ball as though placing a famished cheetah behind an unwary zebra. "One thought: aligned to the target." I align my toes perpendicular to the flag, bend my knees slightly (ha—I had an additional thought and he'll never be the wiser), make sure my spine is straight (that's two additional thoughts—sucker!), then stop. "What if I forget all the other stuff?"

"That's okay," Todd says. "Let your mind wander. One swing thought, get into address, feel the flow through your muscles and just let it all go."

I think of *The Tigger Movie*, Julian's preferred morning entertainment, in particular the scene in which Tigger explains to his young admirer Roo the technique behind his Whoop-de-Dooper, Loop-de-Looper, Alley-Ooper bounce. He rotates his upper frame like a Chinese contortionist, twists his torso several times until it resembles a strand of curled ribbon, coils up his tail as tightly as can be, then releases all that stored energy at once, resulting in a slingshot effect of such velocity that he's able, at least in this case, to dislodge a boulder weighing, well, significantly more than Eeyore and Winnie the Pooh combined. I find myself wondering what kind of golf swing he could put together with that kind of ability. He could make John Daly's takeaway look incomplete.

In fact, I think that's my whole problem. I'm only now realizing it. I don't create enough resistance with the rest of my body to provide opposition for the swing itself. Hm. Why didn't I think of that before? Maybe I did, and I just don't remember. After all, one does have a lot of revelations over the course of his golf career. Can you call something a career if you don't do it professionally? I remind myself to look up "career" versus "hobby" or "vocation." I wonder if other people make an immediate note to look up words if they don't know them. Is it only we writers who do this, because we're so obsessed with always knowing just the right word and so paranoid about not knowing it? What was that idea I had the other day, for that novel? Oh yeah, the thing about the golf pro who's actually a cocaine smuggler, bringing the cocaine in from South America, hidden in golf balls. Wait, is that plausible? How much coke could one really get into a golf ball? Then again, even if it's only a little, a little times many thousands of balls equals a lot. And it's not as though I know how much a golf ball's worth of coke is worth. Could be worth a lot. So it's plausible. I should definitely start that one. Maybe this weekend. Wait, what are we doing this weekend? Julian has a birthday party to go to. No, maybe a wedding—us, not him. Did I ask Mom and Dad to babysit? Wait, maybe he's invited. Wait, is it a bar mitzvah? Yeah, Steph's cousin Michael. Although he's awfully tall for a bar-mitzvah boy. He can't be only 13. Then again, the whole generation is pretty tall. Even the girls. What was the name of that guy in the Guinness Book? Robert Ludlum? No, that's the writer. Robert Laudlow? I'm glad I'm not taller than Dad. Funny that I always wanted to be taller than him. Does every kid want to be taller than his dad at first and then not later? Are most of my friends taller than their dads? Let's see, Ernie is—but maybe that one isn't fair, since his whole family is tall. Man, does he ever look like his brother ... and his mom, too, now that I think about it. That's funny. Genetics is fascinating. Where did I put that letter about the cord blood? Would I have left it on the piano? No, it was important. I must have filed it. Then again, I don't have a file for cord blood. Did I create a file? I don't remember creating a file. I must have left it on the piano. Steph's right, I shouldn't leave mail on the piano. I have to get the piano tuned. Mental note: remember to look up piano tuners.

Robert *Warlow*, was that his name? Man, was he tall. Almost nine feet tall. Would it be fun to be that tall? No way—every piece of clothing would have to be custom-made. I wonder how tall his wife was. Wait, was he married? How the hell did that guy have sex? Then again, as long as you line everything up, what's the difference? But you couldn't do it and kiss at the same time, and kissing takes it to a totally different level. Am I a good kisser? How does one learn to kiss in the first place? Not from what's-her-name in college, that's for sure. And you don't get naked with someone and then tell them they're not allowed to look at your ass. What a mood killer. I'm so glad Julian and Oliver both got Steph's lips. Those are some great lips. So pink. Do girls like big lips on guys? Hey, I just realized the Rolling Stones logo is because of Mick Jagger's lips. That completely makes sense. It's hilarious when you only realize obvious stuff like that way after that fact. Why are the Stones so popular? Then again, I didn't like Springsteen before, and he rules. Maybe I just don't get the Stones. Where's that Springsteen CD? Did I put it in another case? I think I put it in the Duke Ellington case in the car the other day on the way to hockey. That was an okay game, but I have to use a different move on breakaways. Head fake to the short side, then back the other way and over the glove. I should re-tape my stick before the next game. Mental note: buy hockey tape. So funny when Frank freaked out on that guy after the hooking call last week. What did he say? Oh, yeah, *Look at the scoreboard*. That was good. Guy had nothing to say to that.

Maybe Michael *is* only 13. How tall was I at my bar mitzvah? Five-seven, maybe. Pretty tall, not huge. What was the name of that girl in grade eight who said she was the third-smallest baby ever? Lea? Lenore? How many stamps do I have left? They're 51 cents now, right? I think I still have a bunch of fifties. Should I buy some one-cent stamps at the post office, or just wait till I have stuff to mail and buy the extra postage then? I should buy some 51-centers, too, in case I have to mail stuff quickly.

Limor, that was it. Limor Markovski. Didn't I see her walking downtown a few years ago? No, that was Sophie Kourgontopoulus.

If someone asks me who my favorite writer is, I should have an answer ready. Tennessee Williams would be a good answer. Well read but not too pretentious. Or maybe Umberto Eco. Nah—no one ever finishes his books. Salman Rushdie, maybe. That *Seinfeld* episode was so funny. How did they manage to make every single episode funny? Can you say that about any other show? *The Simpsons*, that's the only one. Even *Cheers* had some duds. It's so cute when Julian does cheers with his drinks. Do I let him get away with too much? I don't think I do. You have to let them explore their own boundaries, right? I'm going to read up on that. I shouldn't say "read up"—I'm going to read about that. Should I get Dad a book for Father's Day? What kind of book? Maybe a novel. After all, he never reads novels. Then again, if he doesn't like reading them, why should I force him to? Is a son responsible for keeping his dad sharp as he gets older? Dementia's so weird. Will I know if I'm experiencing dementia, or does dementia by definition mean I won't know I'm experiencing it?

Could she really have been the third-smallest baby ever? What did Miss Duncan say to her that time? Oh, yeah—"Stand up." "I am standing up." That was classic. I guess she could have been third-smallest back then. Now you hear of one-pound babies who survive all the time. They even do fine later on. I shouldn't say later on—that's redundant. Just say later. What are those bolts I have to buy for the towel rack in the bathroom? Topper bolts? Toggle bolts. That's it. How do they work again? Oh, yeah, you feed the thing through the hole, then the wings pop open, then the screw goes through the fixture, then you tighten that side against the other side. Did I charge the drill? I hope I did. I don't remember. I might have. I do remember that when I finished putting that shelf up in the garage it was slowing down, so maybe I charged it then. I can't picture myself doing it, though. Maybe I didn't. I'll find out when I get home. I should hose down the lawnmower and barbecue, too. Then again, does it really matter? It's just a lawnmower. Does it really work any worse if I don't clean it at the beginning of each season? Man, that lawn is tough. I was so into it last summer, and now my heart just isn't there. Should I hire a landscaping service? Maybe it's worth the money. Is that giving up? You could look at it as giving up.

I'd love to get our lawn as green as that grass up there. Boy, do they keep this course nicely groomed. That fairway is impeccable. Is that a ball? That is one beautiful shot. Dead center, look at that. That guy's in beautiful shape. Hit a nice iron from there and he could even get on in t—

"Ahem."

Todd, arms crossed, is grinning at me. I notice that my club seems to have gone from resting on the ground to behind my back, in finishing position. Todd arches his eyebrows in the direction of the drive sitting in the middle of the fairway, then back at me. "Are you going to hit your next shot or stand here admiring that one all day?"

Hm. Apparently, while ruminating about all those things un-related to what I was actually supposed to be doing, I did *that* thing rather well.

Robert *Wadlow*, it occurs to me as Todd and I walk toward my perfect drive.

Strolling toward a glorious shot like this is a quietly rapturous experience, like glimpsing the Taj Mahal over the horizon or hiking toward the Great Pyramids as sunrise breaks. As the imagined, desired thing grows larger in your field of vision, you realize it's as real as the ground you're walking on. It's no dream; it's no illusion. It's there, and it happened, and not only are you here to bear it witness, you were the one who accomplished the feat. As I slide my 7-iron out of my bag, approach the ball and align my toes to the flag once again, I try to remember which king the Pyramids were built for. Ahmenotep? Rameses II? No, he was a pharaoh. That's the same as a king, though. Maybe they just gave their rulers different tags at different times. Or is each pyramid a tomb for a different king? I make a mental note to investigate this ...

The Sweet Spot

The anger produced by a typical golf round—at least, one of my typical golf rounds—will throb intensely before fading sometime between the drive home and breakfast the next morning. Several factors may speed up the fade: remembering an inadvertently funny shot by one of your playing partners; encountering someone less fortunate than you, forcing you to ask yourself, shame-faced, how you can spend any time at all dwelling on a *golf game*; or hearing one of those handful of songs on the radio that always get you, deep down, hitting you in that perfect, soul-filling place no matter how many times you hear them.

Today, even the perfect song isn't helping much. The band is Naked Eyes—fleetingly successful in the mid-eighties before just as quickly disappearing off the face of the earth. I'd admit it to very few, but in the privacy of my own car I'm normally obliged to belt "Always Something There to Remind Me," their one hit, with a childlike smile and momentous anticipation of the drum riff I can execute better than anyone else.

The smile usually prompted by the first note of this tune is barely breaking the surface. Even though I'm singing—when one of those songs comes on, you could be offered a million dollars not to sing along, and the task would be almost impossible—my mouth is producing the melody by rote, with little more than habitual interest. If I were a member of the band, the crowd would say that I'm phoning it in, or at least that my mind is elsewhere. They'd be right. It wasn't that today's golf outing, a 111 (whoever said symmetry is pleasing has never golfed), was worse than any other of my rounds this season; it's *the reason* my game was so bad.

The entire day—every single hole; virtually every single *shot*—was characterized not by my usual lack of focus but by something doubly bizarre: an inability to *stop* thinking. No matter what I tried, I couldn't quit analyzing the shot, the trajectory, my mechanics or the position of the flag (as though this makes a difference to my club selection or swing shape).

Once I became aware this was happening, I was faced with the dual problem of thinking too much and thinking about thinking too much. To say this was out of character is a gross understatement; for me, suddenly becoming an overthinker on the golf course is like a narcoleptic suddenly becoming an insomniac.

Over the course of the round, things only got worse. The more I resisted thinking, the more thinking took hold. By the end of the round I was begging my mind to go blank for one shot just to see how it might turn out. My mind wouldn't oblige. Instead it started forcing me to consider not only the current shot but also the next. I can't even do this in chess; I haven't a clue what gave my brain the idea I might be able to do it on a golf course.

Worst of all, I seem unable to leave it on the course. As the Naked Eyes tune—a truly great classic by a truly great band, even though I may be one of only a handful of people on the planet who realizes it—dies out and the next song begins, I'm ignoring the music and instead replaying shots in my mind, exploring them from every angle, thinking about what I might have done differently. Thinking. I want to unscrew my head and shake its contents out the window.

Only one thing in the world can jolt me from my mental fixation. As I lay in bed that evening, bone tired, about to drift off, my brain using its last snatches of consciousness to question the 4-iron I tried at the seventh, Stephanie shuffles closer, then slides onto my chest. She's feathery and sweet-smelling. I wrap my arms around her and feel the cool skin of her waist. She presses her lips softly to mine. The familiar taste sparks us both. A series of relays clicks and releases inside me, releasing heat in a long, luxurious wave. I smile. On the golf course I may be an involuntary comedian, but I'm an expert where it counts most.

In a whisper Steph asks me something, but I don't quite hear the question. My brain, which I thought had shut down for the night, has become interested in the proceedings. It wants to offer some suggestions. I tell it I'm fine, and it ought to go back to sleep. Instead it asks whether the move I'm using is really the best choice at this juncture. I tell my brain I'm pretty sure Steph likes this move. It asks whether I had a breath mint after the cheeseburger with onions for lunch. My eyes widen. I notice Steph's making kind of a face.

"Is something wrong?" she asks.

"No, everything's fine, everything's great. You're so sexy."

She gives me the grin I love, the grin that is hers alone, the grin that can make me do anything, anytime, that somehow elicits both adoration and lust simultaneously.

I lower my mouth to hers. The effort is somewhat awkward, as though she didn't know the kiss was coming. I'm surprised, since, for the most part, we anticipate and respond to each other's moves like members of a rhythm section seeing chord changes coming several bars in advance.

I change tack, going for her neck instead, just as she turns toward my lips. Her jaw and my forehead collide. I chuckle to show her nothing's wrong, but inside I'm getting uneasy. I go for her mouth again, but this time my lips part as hers close.

I seem to have forgotten how to kiss my wife. This is curious, since I've kissed her a number of times before. Suddenly my tongue feels like it's been added to my mouth overnight. My hands feel clammy. My limbs have become mechanical, as though I'm an ill-constructed robot trying to replicate human movements.

"Doll?" she says. "Are you alright?" We're like two awkward teenagers on a date, but without the giddy anticipation of seeing each other naked for the first time.

"I'm great. I love you."

I try to up the sexy factor by flipping her over, and instead accidentally knee her in the thigh. I plead with my brain to mind its own business. It insists on staying involved. I'm screwed, and not in the good way.

My ardor has turned into a mix of performance anxiety and anger—the same combination I usually experience on the golf course. Then I realize it: the overthinking that took me down on the course today is taking me down in the bedroom tonight.

I won't stand for it. Inability to perform on the links as a result of unnecessary mental participation is one thing—hell, it's expected—but when this tendency tries to creep into the conjugal bed, that's when I draw the line. Or at least I get really ticked off.

"Don't worry about a thing," I tell Steph. "I know exactly what's wrong, and exactly how to fix it." In an attempt to show my mind who's boss, with a bit of seductive flair added, I grab Steph's head and pull it toward me, angling my lips to plant a kiss that will rid both our heads of any capacity for thought. Our teeth knock together. Steph's hand goes to her mouth.

That wasn't very smooth, says my brain.

At dawn the next morning, sexually unsatisfied and matrimonially embarrassed, I switch on the ignition, facing the choice whether to think about my humiliating performance yesterday morning on the golf course or my humiliating performance yesterday evening in bed. I opt to examine the golf humiliation, since it's easier to take and much less surprising.

More important, there's a major difference between poor performance on the links and between the sheets. Every golfer, prior to every round, expects to play better no matter how poorly his previous round has gone. But a lover who has misplaced his touch doesn't cheerfully anticipate his next attempt; he panics that he might have lost it for good. In this way, the recreational golfer has a mental advantage, for in no other sport do participants maintain such persistent optimism without a shred of rational evidence to support it.

Today, I have an extra advantage: I'm wearing a new shirt. My hat and pants are the same as yesterday, but the shirt—forest green with a bit of yellow trim at the sleeves—is crisp and fresh, comfortable and breathable, fresh out of the bag, pins removed, creases ironed. Inspecting myself in the mirror before leaving the house, I could have sworn I was looking at a touring professional.

Midway through the third hole, I'm ready to tear the shirt clear from my body. I've already sliced two drives into the trees and one into water, spectacularly flubbed one fairway wood, rolled off the edge of a green, missed a three-foot putt and taken five shots to get out of two bunkers.

There's a clear, and infuriating, reason for this: I'm thinking again. My brain must have started taking steroids, because it's become not only hyperactive but addicted to its own performance. It's now recommending *two* possible strategies for every shot while I'm at address, neither of which seems right. It's describing various scoring permutations throughout every hole, so I know from shot to shot how all the different possible results of my playing partners' drives, chips or putts might relate to all the different possible results of my own.

It somehow keeps this up for 18 holes, producing a score even uglier than usual, and, for good measure, a pulsing sensation above my left eye. I'm sure it's just a phase, but at the same time I worry that my mind, suddenly so engaged on the golf course, might never learn how to shut itself off again.

I'm doubly nervous returning home. It's evening when I arrive, the house cool and quiet, Julian and Oliver tucked into bed—all the right ingredients for a romantic overture. Steph and I agreed this morning that last night was simply one of those nights. Sometimes you just aren't in sync—and the best, and most fun, way to forget about it is to try again. When I walk in the door, she's got the look.

She removes my hat and giggles at the matted mess underneath. Her fingernails tunnel through my hair as she pushes her little body up against mine. My hands act in reflex, lifting the hem of her shirt toward her ribcage.

"That's more like it," she grins.

"Private Schecter, reporting for duty," I reply. If one of my friends ever told me he'd said this, I'd laugh at him for several days, or perhaps weeks. But when you're in the heat of the moment, just about anything that comes out of your mouth makes you feel like you're writing *The Seducer's Guidebook*.

I hoist her into my arms, carry her up the stairs and toss her onto the bed. (I confess that, after several years of marriage, I still never know whether to hurl her onto the bed from several feet away, flip her gently from a distance of a foot or two, or just sidle up to the mattress and place her down.) She laughs and says, "Get over here."

"That's the plan," I say.

Let's just hope you can perform tonight.

I pause. Did I say that? No. It was inside my head. Oh, for the love of God, I'm thinking again.

What's wrong with thinking? Let's work together. You just take your clothes off, go over there, and I'll talk you through it.

I stop, frozen on the carpet as though suddenly mummified.

"Are you teasing me?" she grins, sitting up. I actually do still have the headache from earlier in the day, but I can't use that as an excuse. She'd never believe it.

Don't worry about yesterday. So you were lousy, big deal. It happens. Forget it. You tried to perform and couldn't. Done. Over. Let's deal with now.

As Steph shuffles to the edge of the bed, takes my hand and pulls me down, I feel I'll be lucky if I can produce even a mechanical response.

Don't rush, murmurs my brain. What does that have to do with anything? Would it have been so hard for God to include an on/off switch, maybe attached behind one of our ears, for moments like these? A simple flick and I'd be all instinct and no thought.

Don't rush, it repeats, even more quietly. On second thought, this isn't bad advice. It's true that my anxiety was making me want to jump the gun a bit.

I slow down. Steph smiles.

Good. No need to hurry it. Slow those hands down.

Slow my hands down? I've heard that somewhere before. I listen—and she likes it.

Okay. Now rotate your hips. Commit to the movement. Go through the full range of motion. Good. Again. Easy, don't rush. Again. Lovely.

My brain, it seems, has become ally rather than adversary. I don't know where this advice is coming from, but the results can't be argued.

Shift your weight smoothly. Don't lunge. That's it, back and forth, back and forth.

Maybe it isn't a change in my brain's allegiance but the simple fact that I'm considering what it has to say rather than dismissing it. Still, the advice feels awfully familiar, as though—

Shift your weight ... back to front, smoothly ...

Wait a minute. This is the same advice it gives me on the golf course. My brain is transferring golf advice to the bedroom.

And it's working.

As Steph's smile grows, I think maybe I should give my brain more credit as a potentially useful contributor both on the golf course and at home. Used judiciously, allowed to participate in moderation, it might just be a valuable tool.

A short time later, Steph rolls off me, her skin glistening. I kiss the back of her shoulder.

"Feeling good?" she says.

"Couldn't be better."

Not only that—I'm suddenly looking forward to my round tomorrow.

Longest Drive?
How About Biggest Slice?

You may have noticed a recent craze sweeping the golf world in which men with thick necks and fearsome swings twist, torque and uncoil their way to fame by launching small, white balls a very long way. Witness the new golf celebrity: the long-drive specialist.

These men have found they can win everything from bragging rights at the local pub to option-loaded SUVs by becoming experts whose skills need not go beyond pulverizing a defenseless Titleist. The long-drive competitor is a unique animal, a one-dimensional titan as interested in learning the rest of the game as Anna Kournikova is interested in learning how to play tennis. Forced to play an entire hole of golf, a champion long-driver might send the ball 390 yards into the middle of the fairway and then botch a 40-yard approach. He might drive the green on a short par 4 but take five shots to get out of the bunker. He might hit drives that make your jaw drop and miss tap-ins Scott Hoch could make.

But he compels us, because he is at once in control yet also the picture of unrestrained fury. When the long-drive behemoth stands at address ready to annihilate another unsuspecting ball, we see every vein in his bulk tensing as though all the energies in the universe are being drawn into his club head. A moment later he becomes the golf equivalent of Tantric sex: supreme focus concentrated down to a quiet center, then unleashed.

We love watching these events the way we love watching horror films. In that silent moment before the assailant's wrath is transferred to the ball, part of us wants to yell, "STOP!" but another part can't wait to see just how much he's going to clobber the thing. And if we're horrified from our sofas, imagine how those Titleists must feel.

In the end, long-drive competitions are, like all such phenomena, transient. Fads emerge, peak and disappear faster than you can say Vanilla Ice. When the popularity of long-drive competitions wanes, the golf world will need to be ready with replacements.

To succeed, these new competitions must offer an element the long-drive competitions, for all their brawny spectacle, don't: they should cater to the fancy of the average golfer. A contest, after all, is only as good as its daydream value, and most duffers can envision themselves winning a long-drive competition about as easily as they can imagine joining the circus.

I've decided to lend my assistance by doing some brainstorming in advance, not that anyone asked. Here are ten replacements for long-drive competitions, representing my very best thinking while wolfing down a tub of Cherry Garcia and watching the *E! True Hollywood Story* of Olivia Newton-John for the seventh time:

1. **Ugly-Swing Open.** The growing popularity of golf has led to a marvelous array of horrendous swings in almost infinite variety. Isn't it time the worst of them were recognized? In this competition, awful swings from all over the world would be judged according to their components—clumsiest backswing, most awkward weight transfer, shoddiest body alignment, most erratic follow-through—as well as for overall hideousness. The contest would be conducted in progressive elimination rounds, followed by a dramatic playoff. *And there's another absolutely repulsive swing. That should give him the lead!* This competition has automatic integrity because, as all players know, you can't fake a bad golf swing any easier than you can correct it. In addition to prize money, the winner would receive the Golf Swing Trainer aid, swing analysis software, the Natural Golf Swing System and a copy of the *Groove Your Swing* CD. Or half a million dollars never to play in public again.

2. **All-You-Can-Eat Invitational.** Competitors play the front nine without food or liquid of any type. At the turn, they get ten minutes to consume whatever they can. Whoever takes in the most calories wins. Viewers would sit captivated as one type of chip gives way to another and players temporarily stop thinking about open club faces to devour open-face clubs. A riveting format because it combines modern athletic fortitude with the primitive instinct to eat and run.

3. **Closest-to-the-Hole Challenge.** Gripping in its simplicity, this competition borrows a page from snooker: sinking the white ball is a no-no. The point here is to get the ball as close to the

hole as possible without sinking it. Since this happens on a regular basis anyway, why not reward those who can do it best?

4. **Tonya Harding Cup.** Reality-show format in which participants are judged on the excuses they come up with for their appalling play. The catch: Competitors are told they've won a free round, but not that they're part of this prestigious tournament. Not until the last putt is made do they realize they've been viewed, and heard, by millions of fans via hidden cameras and microphones placed throughout the course. Imagine the winner's puzzled delight when the host jumps out from behind the bushes and says, *Congratulations! Because you claimed a hamstring contusion on six, ecstasy withdrawal on eleven and West Nile Virus on sixteen, you've won fifty thousand dollars!*

5. **Late-Slice Tourney.** With so many recreational golfers taking to the links today, impressive slices can be found almost anywhere. In fact, a respectable slice practically distinguishes the recreational golfer from everyone else in the world. But it takes true skill to nail a drive that appears good only to swerve left or right near the end of its path. This competition rewards those who can keep their drives straight the longest before banking out of sight forever. Winner receives 20 free golf lessons, a compass and a year's supply of Top-Flite XL3000 Super Straight balls.

6. **Ball-Moving Invitational.** During golf's infancy, the challenge of distracting playing partners while kicking one's ball to a favorable spot was an evolving skill that demanded little creativity *("Is that woman on the tee removing her top?")*. But these days, golfers are more attuned to one another's tricks. In

this exhilarating competition, players attempt to use the foot wedge to knock their balls out of deep divots, thick rough and impossible lies without others seeing. Points are awarded based on the distance the ball is moved and how close other players are when the successful cheater executes his deception. Getting caught entails a stroke penalty and removal of one club from the offender's bag.

7. **Club-Throwing Open.** The sight of a golf ball gracefully cleaving the air is matched only by that of a 3-wood helicoptering down the fairway after its owner has finally snapped. Club throwing is an underappreciated skill whose roots are as old as the game itself, and the best performers are waiting to be discovered (though one must scour the public courses to find them). Points would be awarded not only for distance but also for style. Retired Olympic hammer-throwers would find new jobs as coaches. Prizes would include a free supply of breakable woods and a year's worth of anger management counseling.

8. **Buried-Insult Challenge.** Golf is about more than physical ability. Subtle psychological games have as much influence over a round as whose swing plane follows the right trajectory. Hence the BI Challenge, in which players are awarded points for uttering left-handed compliments meant only to annoy, thereby encouraging one another's games to unravel. We all have a golfing partner who would fare well in this competition. He's the guy who seems to have had formal schooling in the fake compliment intended to irritate. The guy who's always saying things like *Your drive looked so much nicer than mine, but both ended up in the same spot.* The guy you want to brain with a 6-iron.

9. **Speed Golf.** Skins format. Caddies, but no carts. Each golfer has a specific time in which to complete each hole—five minutes for par 3s, eight minutes for par 4s, ten minutes for par 5s. If you think galleries get excited about Tiger lining up a big putt, imagine how they'll react to Colin Montgomerie sprinting down the fairway while frantically checking his watch, or Padraig Harrington looking over a 30-footer as his caddy shouts, *"TEN SECONDS, MAN!"* Besides its inherent amusement, this format would add a positive new element to the tour. Golfers would recruit track coaches to help build their leg muscles. Average course revenues would rise due to the format catching on everywhere and thus more groups moving through. John Daly would adopt a strict cardio training regimen. Note: Speed golf is not recommended for the Seniors Tour.

10. **Wrong-Club Match.** Skins format again, this time with the following wrinkle: Each golfer gets to choose the club the golfer ahead of him uses for every shot, putts excluded. Each club may be chosen only once on a given hole. Imagine Phil Mickelson walloping a pitching wedge off the tee, Ernie Els trying to finesse a 60-yard chip with a 2-iron or Annika Sorenstam studying a downhill pitch-and-run while holding a 5-wood. Who *wouldn't* watch?

A Day at the Abbey

Peering out from the exact spot where Tiger stood, squinting past the lake, trying to make out the green beyond its fortification of trees, I can't bring myself to believe he made this shot. No—I can't believe he *considered* this shot.

As I move my head left and right, still trying to spot the flag—the trees seem to be elbowing up against one another like a group of older kids lacing arms in a game of Red Rover, their expressions just as derisory—I think vaguely of a shot I made a number of years ago at a course I no longer remember.

It was a 3-wood. I couldn't see the hole. I knew Rob and I, with only a few holes left, were within a stroke or two. As I lined up the blind shot, hoping, as always, just to connect well and then let the Gods of Trajectory find the green for me, he said, "You really think you can make this?" It was meant in the spirit of friendly competition, but it was a taunt nonetheless, making it my responsibility either to step up or fail.

A thing happened just then, an irrefutable something in my mind, or maybe my heart, or my guts. Because of this something, I was able, before bringing the club back, to simply look at my friend and smile. I saw his expression change as the ball jumped off my club and flew over the rise beyond us.

"That's a nice golf shot," he said, disappointed. We walked toward the rise, both knowing my ball would be resting on the green when we arrived.

I don't know what happened in that moment just before I swung. I have experienced it numerous times while playing other sports, but only the one time—now more than a decade removed—in golf. Perhaps it occurs when one is so finely focused on the task at hand that the combined force of his concentration and desire can actually dictate the course of action in the universe for a few seconds. Perhaps it comes from the opposite state, a total lack of focus, an unexpected instant of supreme relaxation, every last bit of muscular tension and mental planning slipping pleasurably away as instincts take over, and the body, unencumbered by the mind, simply does what it knows it can do. Or, perhaps, when one's friend tells him he isn't going to make a certain shot, his urge to make it is so powerful that he draws into him the rest of the energies in the galaxy for just an instant, enabling him to do something he shouldn't be able to do.

Everyone in the world who takes part in a sport has experienced such a moment. You were playing basketball with your friends, unsure of your next move, when, suddenly, a moment before it happened, you saw yourself executing the crossover you didn't even know was part of your repertoire. You were in the middle of a game of tennis when you unexpectedly visualized, as clearly as your own reflection, the passing shot you then made an instant later. Or you were standing in the batter's box trying to guess the pitcher's thoughts, when, in a magical flash, guessing turned to a mystical kind of certainty, as though you'd traveled forward in time three seconds, and you saw, a moment before it happened, what was going to occur. You tattooed the pitch, then ran around the bases exhilarated, and slightly disturbed, by the out-of-body moment from which you'd just returned.

Between this moment and my inexplicable 3-wood have come many things. Rob and I are now husbands instead of teenagers. We no longer mow the lawn and take out the garbage to earn our weekly allowance; instead we make mortgage payments and ensure the recycling boxes are properly divided. We don't sling burgers at McDonald's for minimum wage; we have careers, we work hard, we are driven to provide.

But when we look at each other, nothing has changed. We are fourteen years old, it is recess and we have just learned that one of us can throw a tight spiral and the other can catch it. Because of this, we will be friends until we die.

As I stare out past the lake, I remind Rob of my improbable 3-wood.

"Didn't we see a fox?" he says.

So he remembers. As we approached my ball over the rise that day, a gray fox had come trotting casually past us, one moment there, gone the next.

Now, I feel I could more easily make a fox appear out of thin air than make this shot. "I'm lucky if I even reach the lake," I say. "Never mind carry it—*and* the trees ..."

"Give it your best go," says Rob.

Our performances aside, it has been a glorious day. For the first two holes we both played bogey golf, causing us to think, and dare even to mention to each other, that it looked as though we were actually going to shoot 90s at Glen Abbey.

Our shared notion was dispelled at the third, a par 3 over water. Rob skulled his 8-iron, running it just over the edge of the bunker. Feeling good about his shot but forgetting to concentrate on my own, I lifted my head too early, popping up my ball and dropping it straight down into the middle of the lake. Rob tossed me a second ball. I got into address, reminded myself to stay down, and popped it straight up and into the water again. On his own second, intimidated by the huge tongue of lake cutting in front of the green, Rob plopped his directly into the bunker facing him, then his third straight across the green into another bunker fronting the lake, then dribbled his fourth farther into the same bunker, eventually matching my seven.

On the fourth, a manageable par 4, we felt good about our chances again, but only until hitting our tee shots. In my head I must have seen a pitcher trying to throw a fastball past me, because I turned hard on my heels and ripped the ball into the corner—the corner being a cluster of trees to the extreme right of the fairway, forcing me to punch out and settle for yet another seven. Rob's drive made mine look like a work of art, sailing high into the air and then fading far to the left into a fairway bunker, which he took three shots to exit. He then putted back and forth on the green for a while, talking to himself a little more with each putt, eventually coming away with a nine.

I could tell he knew it was a horrendous score by the way he looked back over the hole from the green, counting his shots. Anytime a golfer does this, one may automatically add a stroke to whatever he calculates. Every golfer has, hardwired into his head, a mechanism that conveniently eliminates one, sometimes two, strokes from memory when they are being counted at the end of a hole.

"Eight," he said.

"Sorry," I was forced to say, "I'm pretty sure it's a nine. You were two to the fairway bunker, three out, on the green in six ..."

"Oh, yeah," he replied. It isn't a conscious desire to cheat that causes all golfers to do this; it's the desperate desire to let our unconscious do the cheating for us so that we might still be able to look at ourselves in the mirror the next morning.

The perspective for our tee shot on six was one of the most wide open I've ever seen. For 200 yards nothing stood between us and the fairway except immaculately groomed farmland.

"I'm looking forward to seeing how I'm going to mess this one up," I said to Rob, then promptly answered the question by topping my drive right, eating up maybe 30 of those 200 yards. After muscling a 5-wood toward the 150 stick on my second shot, I saved bogey by accidentally draining a long putt, starting it right, just getting over a ridge, then curving it down into the cup—even though, as testament to the amateur's poor eye and poorer feel, as the ball started its roll about ten feet away, I shouted, "No!"

On the par-4 eighth, we both mashed our drives to the center of the fairway. I then cuffed my 5-iron, getting lucky when it rolled all the way to the edge of the green. Rob, grabbing the other side of the luck stick, hit his solid but watched it fall just short and roll down into a starfish-shaped bunker half the size of my backyard. We both carded sixes. When we reached the next tee, he turned in a sprint back toward the previous green, saying, "I told myself, *Don't forget the club, don't forget the club.*"

We'd scored 58 and 56, respectively, on the front half. The starter had told us this was the more open, more forgiving half, the section preceding the valley holes, after which things, he said, would "get tougher," his expression changing as though advising us how to play the back nine in hell.

The Abbey truly does prove to be two courses in one. The holes before the valley—broad, straight and littered with bunkers—demand intelligent, but not precise, play. A riveting contrast, the valley holes require precision and a flair for inspired shotmaking. In other words, we were screwed on both counts.

No matter how terrifically bad we were playing, it was impossible not to appreciate the course's aesthetic. On the Abbey's signature hole, 11, we stood atop the high plateau gazing into the valley as though into a beautiful kingdom of doom. From this panorama one feels like an ancient invader planning a secret attack from above.

Reality reverses this perception. The hole, beginning a stretch that has reduced more than one PGA touring professional to tears, attacked us without prejudice. Looking down over the valley at a variety of trees, one solitary weeping willow tucked among them (which I feared might be symbolic), then, beyond the bunkers, a creek, then, beyond it, players as small as ants starting toward the next hole, you feel the green is about as close, and about as accessible, as the horizon.

Just in case you feel comfortable with your tee shot, the spirit breaking steps up later by revealing the depth illusion you've just fallen for. No matter how you might have crushed it from the plateau, after riding the cart down the steep hill, emerging out of the trees and locating your ball, you inevitably hear only one question in your head. *How is there still so much left to the green?*

As you proceed through, desperate to resurface as though flailing underwater and kicking hard for the surface, the valley holes continue their happy deception. You're constantly hitting what you think are impressive drives only to find you still have miles to the green, or facing impossible decisions whether to lay up or try to carry water, both decisions ultimately calamitous.

After making our way through the valley about as elegantly as a surfer trying to fight through pack ice, we re-emerged, our earlier notions of bogey golf long dismissed. At the par-4 seventeenth, wide open again, we were treated to what felt like a panorama of sand, as though we'd suddenly fallen asleep and awakened in the Sahara. My quick scan of the fairway revealed no fewer than ten bunkers, with at least three more immediately visible on the way to the hole. Between us Rob and I couldn't avoid visiting about a third of them, as though the green was our hometown and the bunkers relatives we were forced to stop in and see along the way.

Now, standing in the very trap where Tiger once stood, I try to summon the magical visualization that allowed me to smoke that 3-wood so long ago, knowing one can conjure the magic no more easily than he can will a ten-foot putt into the center of the cup.

Most amazing is that Tiger didn't need magic to pull this off. All he needed was grit, confidence, the spotlight focused squarely on him and—incredibly—a 6-iron.

During his sensational two-year run to open the twenty-first century of golf, when it seemed he obliterated the fields of every tournament from the Masters to the Greater Hartford Open to the Tour de France, he had come to the eighteenth at the Canadian Open a stroke up on a New Zealander named Grant Waite, who was slightly lesser known than Tiger the way my third-grade family portrait is slightly lesser known than the *Mona Lisa*.

Tiger's tee shot found a sand trap on the right edge of the fairway, the trap in which I now stand. Waite hit a safe 223-yard approach to the fat part of the green, leaving himself a long putt, but on in two nonetheless. Tiger would have to punch out or lay up.

At least, that's what the rest of the world thought. He took the 6-iron, twisted his heels into the sand, looked up a last time, perhaps knowing, just as I had that day in the past, what was going to happen next, and pulled the trigger. The gallery's roar, swelling with tentative anticipation at first, grew to the thunderous levels reserved only for mass disbelief as the ball found first the air over the lake, then the space beyond the tops of the trees, then, as if a guided missile, began its descent, striving for the green like a long-jumper squeezing out every last precious inch, and dropped, eventually, onto a spot 18 feet past the flag. From there Tiger matched Waite's birdie to earn his ninth title of the year and place his Canadian Open victory alongside the national titles of the U.S. and Great Britain, in the process causing an endless parade of superlatives for days afterward.

I waggle my 6-iron one last time. I look up, picturing the shot. In this case, what I picture is my ball catching the lip of the bunker. I shake that image out of my brain and demand another. This time it offers a short film of the ball flying straight up into the air and coming straight back down.

Maybe pressure will help. I picture the scene that surrounded Tiger: the packed gallery, its collective breath held in anticipation; Waite, wondering just how deep Tiger's guts ran; the rest of the field, waiting to see what trick the man might be conceiving in his head.

I bring the club back, start my hips forward and slash wickedly at the ball. My extra-tight grip and knack for misalignment combine to push the clubhead left, causing the ball to jump off the toe of the club. The good news is I get out of the bunker easily; the bad news is the ball goes 45 degrees left of where I'd intended. It bounces cheerfully across the fairway, finally deciding to rest on the left edge.

"Tiger would be proud," Rob says, stepping up for his attempt. We've agreed to try the shot once each no matter where our actual tee shots land. A longer hitter than me, he has a better shot at this. He should also, by now, have much more skill around the sand. Since we started playing local nine-hole courses as teenagers, he has displayed a bizarre and unremitting talent for finding sand on a golf course. Though I haven't kept precise count today, I know he has found at least a dozen traps, several of them at the end of respectable drives or decent approach shots.

Though Rob catches his shot cleanly, he actually only succeeds in demonstrating the ridiculousness of the actual shot we're trying to replicate. Rob's ball, though struck about as well as he could strike it, flies out to the middle of the lake and dies, sending up a harmless splash.

Between the spot where Rob's ball runs out of juice and the spot where Tiger's ball landed, there lie perhaps 150 yards. Before resuming play with our actual shots (mine a foot into the woods on the left, his two feet in), I pause a moment, staring at the path of Tiger's shot to comprehend it as much as my brain will allow. I find I'm shaking my head back and forth.

Rob grins. "No matter how long you stand here, you're never going to believe it."

"You're right—I don't."

We finish our rounds, quickly adding our scores and then agreeing never to speak of them again. No galleries cheer us as we bend to remove our balls from the cup. No photographers are waiting to snap our pictures, no fans wanting us to sign their programs, no oversized checks awarded. Our golf world is quiet and self-contained, our shots captured for posterity only in our own eyes and transmitted not to millions of avid fans but mostly back and forth to each other. It is a world where the most repeated stories are those involving not shots that have drawn our admiration but those that have made us laugh the longest or hardest. The most important thing about our golf world isn't golf itself, but the fact that we have each other in it.

Ira's 80

You know why I like my friend Ira? He would never lie to me about his golf score. I have some other friends who regularly lie about their scores, and, while I'm not going to name names, it's all of them.

Ira just doesn't operate that way. That's why, when I get wind of the news he recently shot 80, I figure it's probably true, but I still want to know the details. If certain other of my friends told me they'd scored 80, I'd assume it was actually 88, or perhaps that they were on drugs.

I call Ira on a Sunday night. His wife, Elisa, answers. She tells me he returned from a weekend fishing trip an hour ago and fell asleep instantly. He's definitely knocked out till morning. I ask her to wake him up. Ira and I go back a while.

"Hello?" He's groggy.

"Hey, it's me. So is it true?"

"What, about the pickerel? It was only five pounds. What's the big deal?"

"No, about the 80."

"Look, I'm only about five percent awake here."

"The 80 at Copper Creek. True?" He pauses, because he knows I shouldn't have to ask. "Okay, I'll warm you up. Where'd you fish?"

"I think it was called Kamiskaming."

"With whom?'

"Elisa's brothers."

"Do you smell like fish?"

"Not really. There weren't many around." He yawns. "Why do you care about the 80?"

"I'm writing a golf book."

"I know that."

"I want to include this."

"Why?"

"Because."

"No argument."

"When was the round?"

"I would say, let's see, July, the long weekend. Canada Day weekend. No, I'm going to say second week of July. I'm not really sure. This is going to be some interview."

"Don't worry about that. Who did you play with?"

"Eric, Addy and Mike. No, Eric, somebody else and Mike. Jay. Was that his name? Jason. Friend of Mike's. The guy didn't crack a smile the whole day. He was weird."

"When did you know it was a special round?"

"I guess when I, let's see, I think it was when I ... not until the fourteenth hole. Second birdie in three holes. Then I knew something was up."

"How well did you think you were doing?"

"I knew it had the potential to be my best round, because there were no really bad holes. Lots of bogeys, but no doubles or triples."

"What was your best previous round?"

"I don't know, 87, maybe. Can I go back to sleep now?"

"Did you use your driver?"

"For four holes—but I was hitting it so bad, I put it in the bag and kept it there. That's when I started sizzling."

"See, that's a great sound byte—*That's when I started sizzling.* You're a natural interview subject. Were you counting shots going into the final holes?"

"I purposely didn't. Mike and Eric kept asking me if I wanted to know my score, which obviously told me I was doing well, but I kept saying no. Man, am I tired. Lots of guys shoot 80. Why interview me?"

"I know you."

"Unfortunately."

"What were your impressions of Copper Creek?"

"It's beautiful. I don't know, lots of different kinds of holes, perfect conditions. I don't know. What kinds of things do you want me to say?"

"Whatever you want to say."

"Okay, it's really nice to the eye and it's just, I don't know, fairways are immaculate, bunkers are nice. Look, you're the stupid writer."

"What was your worst shot of the day?"

"Actually, it was on a hole I eventually birded. I hit an awful 3-wood off the tee, but it happened to land in an opening. My approach stuck on the edge of the green, then I sank a 40-foot putt. That'll happen again within about ten years if I'm lucky."

"What would you consider the strongest part of your game?"

"That's a tough one. I would say my mid-irons. Not that any part's particularly strong."

"Weakest part?"

"Putting."

"Why?"

"Because I suck at it."

"Why do you suck at it?"

"Because I can never hit the ball in the direction I want. Especially with straight putts. They're impossible. It's like pool. Give me a putt that breaks over a straight one every time."

"What would you say is the most common golf flaw?"

"Buying expensive clubs when they aren't going to make a difference."

"That's not really what I was after."

"I thought I could say what I want. Hey, here's a good saying I heard during that round: The bad golfer plays again for the one good shot he's made, the good golfer plays for the one bad shot."

"I don't get it."

"If you're a bad golfer you want to recapture the one good shot you made, and if you're a good golfer you want to correct the one bad shot. It kind of loses impact if I have to explain it to you."

"Did you hit any spectacular shots during the round?"

"It wasn't that I was spectacular. More like I managed not to give shots away. If I made a bad shot, I was able to resist making a dumb next shot. That usually isn't the case."

"I know, I consider you quite dumb. Okay, you can go back to sleep. I was just curious."

"Are you sure this is important enough to put in your book?"

"Look at it this way: I don't know anyone who's ever shot 79."

Michael's 79

When first introduced, hairstylist and client inevitably play a mutual game in which each silently asks himself the same question about the other: *Is he a talker?*

I have no idea whether the stylist's preferred answer is yes or no, since I've never been a stylist. I imagine this must depend on day, hour and mood, just as it does for the client. Sometimes you'd welcome 30 minutes of predictable dialogue; sometimes you'd be just as happy to sit quietly with your own thoughts or flip through the issue of *In Style* that's 16 months out of date.

How often do the conversational inclinations of stylist and client match? Again, I have no idea, since I've existed on only one side of the equation. But I do know that it takes just one or two visits for both to determine the typical habits of the other.

With Ray at Franco's Salon and Spa, it took only one visit. That was three years ago. I now know to expect a steady flow of conversation from the moment I set foot in the salon until the moment

I leave. Built like a linebacker with a face like Valentino, Ray inspired in me plenty of negative assumptions. But where I expected arrogance and machismo, I instead encountered sweetness and sensitivity. The guy is Florence Nightingale in a Latin mask.

Now, our conversations having progressed from the necessary initial phase of *Do you live around here?* and *Seen any good movies lately?* to stuff actually relating to our particular lives, I consider Ray a friend. While I don't know much about him, I know a few critical things. He has a teenage son, Adrian, whom he is trying to stay close to during the period when kids often shut out their parents for reasons even they don't know. He adores young children, evidenced by the way he'll interrupt my haircut to twirl Julian in the next chair and say things like "That fun, buddy?" He likes and respects women. He pays attention to what people say, so that, when I come in mid-afternoon on a weekday, Julian in tow, he doesn't have to ask me for the fifth time what I do for a living, and instead asks whether I'm taking a break before finishing the current manuscript. And, after all, I see him every five or six weeks, which is more often than I see some of my closest friends.

Wandering into The Men's Salon Hairstyling and Barbershop, I feel like I'm cheating on Ray—though the need for this visit is obvious to anyone not living in a cave. Working downtown for the past two months helping the senior executives of a multinational corporation write sentences their shareholders can actually understand, I've become a regular office dad—gone at sunrise, home for dinner. Because I haven't had time to see Ray on the weekend, I've sailed past official scruffy territory and am now entering the land of hirsute. The werewolf hair on my neck is starting to threaten an appearance above my shirt collar. My sideburns are getting so bushy they belong in a disco ballroom. If I don't get a cut soon, the next Bigfoot sighting will feature a photo of me.

The laminated sign on the reception desk informs me that The Men's Salon is distinguished by its proud adherence to old-school principles: warmed shaving cream thumbed into the sideburns and back of the neck, straight blade for the shave, hot towel to soothe the skin. I don't want to feel old, but I don't mind old school.

I'm introduced to Michael, a trim, spectacled, owlish-looking gent, probably mid-forties, who greets me with a pleasant British accent. Michael could be the guy who runs your local library, but there's a glint in his eye that lets me know he probably isn't loath to share a dirty joke as well.

Settling into the chair, I try to decide whether Michael is a talker. We run through the normal battery of questions—he asks me if I work nearby; I tell him I'm on contract for a bit; we agree the weather has been splendid; he asks me whether we're going for the full shearing, the minor clean-up or something in between, I make the joke that we need to go short enough that I can feel the breeze on my neck but not so short that my wife will salute me when I get home. None of this really tells us what we want to know, since everyone does this as a matter of course. It is at this point that stylist and client agree either to mutual silence, patchy conversation or sustained dialogue.

Soon, I realize the guessing game isn't necessary. As Michael's scissors begin to dart in and out, his comb flashing between my hair and his fingers, I realize he has a buzz on. It isn't a buzz induced by alcohol, but by something else. He's practically humming as he peers at one side of my head or the other, snips a few small rows of hair, inspects me in the mirror, then continues.

My mental game shifts to guessing what has put the bee in Michael's bonnet. Did he win big in his poker game last night? See an inspiring sunset? Get lucky? I don't know if I'm feeling talkative or if I'm just too curious not to ask, so, as tiny hairs fly past my eyes, I come out with it: "You seem chipper."

Michael pauses, steps back, places the hand holding his comb on one hip and the hand holding his scissors on the other, and then his reflection says to mine, "I've been golfing for almost 30 years. Last weekend, the most amazing thing happened." His face takes on an expression of astonishment, as though he himself can't believe the thing he's referring to.

Even were I to have less interest in writing about golf than the mating rituals of dung beetles, I'd still be interested in this. It's always nice to learn about others having positive golf experiences, the same way it's pleasurable to watch others having sex even when one isn't enjoying much of it himself.

"When I started playing," he says, "I got a set of persimmon clubs. I never changed them until a few months ago, when I switched to some graphite-shafted clubs with titanium heads." You can tell he enjoys saying *graphite-shafted clubs with titanium heads*.

"Persimmon? Seriously?"

"Never used any others."

"You're English?"

"Scottish. But I moved to England at four and grew up there. Anyway, I'm not a long hitter. Plus, you're talking to a 62-year-old man. So these clubs were really holding me back."

"Sixty-two? You look 42."

"Thanks, chap. Try to take care of myself. After I traded in the persimmons, I gained some yards and started playing a little better. Last week I was out with my brother-in-law and a friend of mine.

Both pretty good players. Barry shoots in the 80s, Grant in the 90s. I usually average about 95. I'd played 17 times this year, and only six times broken a hundred. Well, I started—"

"Wait!" I say to Michael. "How long is my haircut going to take?"

He looks puzzled. "Half-hour. Maybe a little more."

"I don't want to know the ending yet."

He looks at me suspiciously.

"I want to know the backstory. Do you come from a golfing family?"

He pauses, slowly resumes cutting, and says, "No. Dad never played a sport, sister never played a sport. Golf wasn't in the blood. I didn't even pick up the game until I was 34." His scissors pick up a bit of speed. "A friend in England introduced me to it."

"What did you play growing up?"

He steps back from the chair again, adjusts his glasses and looks at me in the mirror. "Rugby. Oh, I would love to have played rugby at a high level. Or soccer, or tennis. But I was too small for rugby. Tried it as a 16-year-old and promptly got four teeth knocked out. That didn't impress Dad. So really I took up golf because I was no bloody good at anything else."

"What brought you here?"

"To the salon?"

"To the country."

"My wife. Her family's from Windsor—"

"Ontario?"

"England. But she was born in Toronto. I met her in England, we planned to come here for a year and see how it worked out. Twenty years later, here I am."

"Do you remember your first impressions of Canada?"

Michael whisks some hairs from my face. "Certainly. I remember thinking two things: everything's bigger, and everything's cleaner."

"What's going through your mind when you're standing over your ball? What do you feel?"

"Trepidation, mostly."

"How about when you catch one just right?"

"Ohhhh," he sighs, as if I've slipped him a sedative. "You don't even feel it. When you hit it off the screws, and you get your lower body involved, and you're right on plane ..." Michael steps back from the chair and performs a slow-motion swing, eyes closed, smile huge. The scissors and comb come through the impact zone. "I tend to go outside the ball. I get my wrists cocked on the backswing, and I hang on and hang on, instead of releasing."

"Hey—you're a leftie?" I ask.

"You're looking in the mirror," he says. So I am. "I learned to cut hair right-handed. That's why I ended up golfing from that side."

Maybe it's because of the pleasurable sensation of the buzzer on my neck, but I'm enjoying this spontaneous interview. I bet if you asked the top 50 golfers on the tour why they swing one way or another, not many of them would attribute the preference to having learned to cut hair from that side.

"Where would you say that feeling of hitting one just perfectly ranks among the greatest sensations?" I ask. "And could you even out my sideburns?"

"No problem. I'd say it ranks, let's see, among the top ten. Behind single-malt whiskey, classical music, children's laughter or the sound of birds singing."

Ah, the oldest archetype in literature: the golf-obsessed English male hairstylist with a sensitive side. "Okay. Now take me back. You replace the persimmons, buy the new clubs, and then ..."

"I'm out there with Barry and Grant, course called Country Lane, and I decide to leave the driver in the bag on the first tee. I strike one well. It's going to be a good day." Michael warms some shaving cream, takes a small quantity on each thumb and massages it into my sideburns and the back of my neck. The sensation is gorgeous. I close my eyes and smile. "Soon, I realize I'm making all the shots. This was somebody else hitting the ball."

He washes the straight blade, flicks off the excess water with a beautiful wrist motion, then leans in and performs a series of expert scrapes. "It continues like that the whole round. My driver never sees the light of day. I don't want to be keeping score, but I can't help it. I get to 17 knowing that if I birdie the last two, I'll hit 79." He lays a hot towel over my face. "Seventeen's a par 5. I go 3-wood off the tee, then 3-wood again, then 5-iron, which sticks at about 20 feet. So I've lost the opportunity, but I gave it my best shot, which is all you can ask for. Then something wondrous happens. I sink the bloody thing."

From under the towel I say, "I think I know what's coming."

Michael beams. "On 18, par 4, it's 3-wood again off the tee. Right down the heart of the fairway. I'm in perfect position. I take my 5-wood out of the bag. Just get it on the green is all I'm thinking. It sails out there, bounces and rolls to three feet of the hole." He removes the towel.

"Three feet?"

"I felt like I'd died and gone to heaven. I sink the putt for birdie. Seventy-nine. I still don't believe it." Michael angles a mirror to my neck so I can inspect it, then unsnaps my cape and shakes it out. "You're done, my friend."

"That was a heck of a good story," I say, handing him a tip.

"Thanks for listening."

"See you in a month."

I've never gone the straight blade and hot towel route before; now, I don't think I can ever go back. Not to mention that few haircuts in my life have been this enjoyable. Thanks to Michael's 79, I've had 30 minutes of entertainment without having to do much in return. And as a fellow hacker, I'm truly thrilled for him. No matter what he does for the rest of his golfing life, he'll always have the round when he caught lightning in a bottle.

And if he caught it, then one day, maybe, just maybe, I can, too.

Easy Ryder

Though the Ryder Cup trophy stands a mere 17 inches tall and weighs barely four pounds, grown men battle for it with greater zeal than teenagers clamor for the latest *Harry Potter*. The event transcends its own stature as a golf contest. Watching the Ryder, one senses that the jousters and soldiers of old have morphed into more admirable form, lances and muskets transformed into woods and irons, suits of armor and red coats exchanged for khakis and collared shirts adorned with little alligators or Nike swooshes.

The Ryder appeals to us in ways other sports can't. Attending a given soccer match means consenting to better-than-average odds of watching players being trampled, or at least being inadvertently kneed in the groin. Olympic track and field features athletes so jacked up on steroids their muscular striations spell out *Inject here*. The greatest violence that might occur in a Ryder gallery is one person's shoe accidentally scuffing another's and, though fitness has come to play a prominent role in golf, we can still be fairly unconcerned about whether John Daly is taking muscle-enhancing drugs.

There's the wonderful pressure (wonderful because we get to enjoy it from our sofas), the unparalleled excitement that unfolds from the first drive to the last putt. It has been said that making a four-foot putt to win a Ryder match is more nerve-racking than making a ten-footer to win a major. Imagine the butterflies you feel lining up a gimme to steal a skin from your fellow hackers, then multiply those butterflies by the entire population of Europe or America, and you begin to appreciate what these pros feel.

Do they do it for personal glory or riches? No—the Ryder is compelling because it is driven purely by the spirit of competition and love for a game that has become as universal as an irreparable slice. No jaw-dropping checks change hands, no green jackets are presented; that pint-sized trophy awarded at tourney's end is the sole prize. (The golfer atop the trophy isn't even Ryder himself; it's his friend and instructor, Abe Mitchell. Unless Tiger, Monty and the others harbor a secret desire for a statue of Mr. Mitchell, these guys must be in it for the right reasons.)

It's no coincidence that Samuel Ryder was a fixture at both Stratford-on-Avon's golf club, where the tournament was born, as well as its Shakespearean festivals. Killing some hours on the course prior to enjoying the theater, Ryder, though he couldn't have sensed it at the time, created the most gripping marriage of golf and drama we know today. No doubt he would have enjoyed the recent film *Miracle*, about the U.S. hockey team's improbable gold at the 1980 Olympics, in which coach Herb Brooks tells his players they won't succeed until recognizing that the name on the front of the jersey means more than the one on the back.

In other words, the Ryder is what competition should be all about. Though only one side gets to hoist that little trophy in the end, it is we fans who truly win.

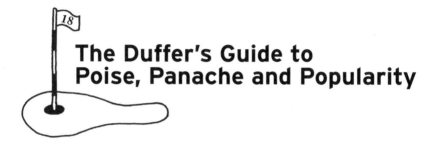

The Duffer's Guide to Poise, Panache and Popularity

In golf, there are the elite, and then there are the rest of us. We others, lumped together in the Duffer Zone—you know us from the formal announcements we send out whenever we break 100—are like the thousands who finish mid-pack in a big-city marathon: happily unremarkable, content just to enjoy the sunshine with some like-minded others, unconcerned about the guy who crossed the tape 40 minutes earlier.

We are competent but not brilliant. We are enthusiastic, though a far cry from intense. Our fairway woods are mostly reliable, but put a 3-iron in our hands and we might as well be swinging a screwdriver.

This is by no means a disadvantage. While top golfers spend countless hours examining their swing plane, wrist hinge, hip turn and Big Bertha head size in the desperate attempt to shave a stroke or two, we can call it an agreeable day if our cart has good pickup. Moreover, since the odds of us putting together a stellar round are as high as that of Charles Barkley winning a major, we don't agonize over the fact. We understand perfectly well that improving one's game by tiny increments is as easy as swimming the English Channel in a suit of armor, so we celebrate our pars, take our double-bogeys in stride and get on with things.

That said, even if those of us in the Duffer Zone don't turn heads with our game (except when hollering "Fore!", which we do with such frequency that each of us has his own unique sound, kind of like a mating call), it still behooves us to act respectably on the course. After all, there's unremarkable and then there's embarrassing. Finishing a marathon out of the top group is one thing, but doing so while wearing a headband and knee-highs is another. So even if you aren't likely to birdie the twelfth at Augusta anytime soon, you can still conduct yourself in an admirable manner. Here are ten ways.

1. **Leave the tam-o'-shanters to real Scotsmen.** The late Payne Stewart was entitled to wear traditional knickers because he was a successful touring pro. Jesper Parnevik can pull off outlandish jumpers and tipped-up brims since he can also hit a 1-iron. Jack Nicklaus was well within his rights to wear those horrendous plaid pants because he was in the process of winning his sixth Masters at the time. Until you have similar credentials or Nike offers you an endorsement deal, stick with plain khakis or chinos, understated tops, and hats that don't bear the names of construction companies. Once you're carding below 85 regularly, feel free to break out the salmon or kelly green shirts. And if you're shooting under 80, wear whatever the heck you want.

2. **Save the flimsy excuses for when you forget your anniversary.** There's no shame in being a poor golfer. But that doesn't mean you should draw unnecessary attention to it. If your game is lacking, you're merely in the same boat as millions of others, so there's no need to overcompensate with statements like, "I just don't have it today," "That pin position was impossible," "My ex-girlfriend put a curse on me" or "What a rotten time for my thoracic hypoplasia to act up." Substitute your excuses with more strategic remarks, like, "So who do you like more, Halle Berry or Jessica Alba?", which will get your partners focused on much more important things than your golf-related defects. It may help bring their scores a lot closer to yours, too.

3. **Remind yourself that if you didn't know how to hit a draw before the round, it's unlikely you're going to discover how to hit one during it.** In other words, don't try to experiment too madly. If you don't usually hit your 5-iron more than 160 yards, there's no reason to expect you're going to spontaneously hit it 20 yards farther on a crucial shot, even if your instinct is telling you something different moments prior to the backswing. Stick with what you know, even if what you know consists of the occasional solid mid-iron and little else. It's far better than trying something complicated and looking like a cross between Charlie Chaplin and Jack Tripper in the attempt.

4. **Hit one long putt, great chip or improbable bunker save during the round.** Just as you remember the one straight flush you had in an otherwise abysmal night of poker, one brilliant play, intentional or not, can overshadow a generally appalling round. So, while I realize that telling you to hit one outstanding

shot is a bit like telling you to get Jennifer Lopez's private pager number, it's worth its weight in gold if you can manage it. After all, the main advantage of being an erratic golfer is that, while great golfers tend to hit 80 solid, controlled, low-risk shots, the kind of swing that produces a score of 100 also tends to produce one or two inadvertently tremendous balls. You're obligated to try. Prayer never hurts, either.

5. **Hit one spectacularly bad shot during the round.** Much easier, and doubly valuable, than hitting one great shot is hitting one shot that puts everyone in stitches. Just as every foursome needs someone to tell good jokes and keep spirits light, it also needs someone who can pull out a mind-warping slice, laser-through-the-grass tee shot or bunker-to-bunker chipping sequence to break the tension at a critical juncture. Be that guy. It shouldn't be too hard.

6. **Think more Dalai Lama, less John Daly.** Golfers who maintain equanimity on the course command respect if not for their game then at least for their composure. Don't curse your shanks three holes after they've been forgotten by everyone else. Don't take half a dozen mulligans on each nine. And don't spend endless minutes searching for your errant drives deep in the heart of out-of-play territory. (Rule of thumb: When the squirrels start calling you by name, you're taking too long to look for your balls.) Besides, deep down we all know that sending our fairway wood twirling into the nearest tree isn't going to make us feel any better. Okay, it might make us feel better, but it isn't going to impress our boss, father-in-law or anger management coach.

7. **Practise the fundamentals.** Every recreational golfer in the world faces the same challenge: trying to achieve at least something resembling a sound golf swing. Don't try to replicate Sam Snead's stroke right away. First, get a handle on the little things. For example, try not to start admiring your drives before you actually make contact with the ball. Keep your front arm straight instead of letting it relax like a piece of string. And remember that putting all the parts of a swing together coherently goes a lot further than blasting your pecs and biceps. Davis Love III doesn't hit the ball far because he's built like an air mattress; he hits it far because of good mechanics. If brute strength automatically translated into low scoring, that guy at my gym who presses four plates on either side would top the PGA money list and Mike Weir would be his caddy.

8. **Play like you mean it.** Sure, a golf swing seems more complicated than the Special Theory of Relativity at the best of times. But, like that of a student resolved to conquer trigonometry or die trying, your effort can be its own reward. A baby not yet able to walk still gets praise for trying. In other words, giving it your best, even if your best entails a potential score higher than your university professor's IQ, will still win you kudos.

9. **Be the fun guy.** Can you hit a 7-wood? Maybe not. But if you can regale them at the nineteenth with humorous anecdotes and obscure Super Bowl trivia, who cares? The fun guy is always more in demand than the guy who can hit it a mile, the guy with the textbook swing or the guy whose wife looks like Pamela Anderson. So while your buddies are reading *Ben Hogan's Five Lessons*, *David Leadbetter's Faults and Fixes* or *Dave*

Pelz's Putting Bible, spend some time with *Truly Tasteless Jokes, The Complete Book of Zingers* and *A Funny Thing Happened on My Way Through the Bible,* and see whose drinks are covered at the end of the round.

10. **Know the game.** A bad gardener can pass himself off as Mr. Green Thumbs by talking intelligently about perennials, soil composition and fertilizer grade. A terrible basketball player is likewise perceived more favorably if he can rhyme off Michael Jordan's career stats or dissect the reasons behind Villanova's upset over Georgetown in the 1985 NCAA Finals. In the same vein, knowing your loft angles, shaft materials and ball compression levels can make it seem like you have all the requisite knowledge to become a master of the links. That you aren't capable of applying that knowledge is insignificant, at least in the grand scheme.

And here's a bonus tip: bring plenty of balls. When someone hits his last one into the drink and even the longest telescopic ball retriever isn't up to the task, the guy who can provide an extra sleeve is like a messiah in herringbone.

Till Death Do Us Par

The first time, I was 17. It was a third cousin on my mom's side, whom I'd met only a handful of times. I can't remember her name. In fact, I remember little more than getting dressed up, having a few drinks I wasn't old enough to have and then watching her enter. I didn't even really notice the activity around me. She looked beautiful—angelic, almost. Like everyone, I couldn't take my eyes off her. It all seemed to happen in slow motion.

The next time, I was more familiar with the way everything worked—what was supposed to happen when—and so my eyes wandered a bit. She was my boss, so I couldn't say no, but the honest truth was I'd rather have been out with my friends. A few times I noticed the people in the distance and what they were doing. I didn't have any great urge to be doing the same, since I wasn't into that sort of thing yet—but I noticed. For her sake, I pretended to be interested for a few hours, then headed home. It was late, my ears were ringing, my head was pounding, I needed sleep. I didn't remember much about the afternoon and evening, though there did seem to be, flickering in the back of my mind, images of the competition that had been transpiring around us.

As I got older, it started happening more. There was the quickest one, involving a friend from school; the steamiest, on a muggy evening in late August, amid the chirping of crickets and a semi-circle of tiki torches; the hardest to endure, due to food poisoning; and the most strangely compelling, with my friend Laurence, his soon-to-be-wife Collette and, in honor of her native heritage, burning sweetgrass.

There was the one up north, the one in New York, the one in Montreal. Each involved different people—and in each case my attention would shift, just a little more than the previous time, from the events at hand to those happening just beyond. It was almost surreal, since what we were doing and what they were doing had no connection. We all just happened to be using the same space.

Now, here I am again. It isn't that I don't feel ecstatic for my cousin, Alex, and his bride, Catherine. They're the kind of couple— madly in love, cool as cucumbers, all freckles and smiles—whose permanent oath to each other you feel privileged to witness. It isn't that I don't want to appreciate them as they exchange their vows up there on the grass. It's that I can't believe the guy 50 feet behind them just blew that three-foot putt.

In the interest of honesty, perhaps I should send a note to every couple I know who might have me on their wedding list, to tell them that, if the wedding is to be held at a golf or country club, they shouldn't waste a seat on me. Instead of turning to watch the bride when she comes down the aisle, I'll be watching the action on the green behind the officiant. Rather than cutting a rug on the dance floor, I'll be sneaking out for a better look at the eighteenth fairway. The flowers and centerpieces will be lost on me because I'll be preoccupied by thoughts of aprons and fringes.

I'm quite serious about this. Look, I don't *want* to be absent at the weddings of my closest friends and family members. I love weddings. And away from golf courses, I'm a great guy to have at them. I'm a male softie with hair-trigger tear ducts who isn't afraid to discuss the subtleties of chair covers and napkin-fold styles. But if little white balls are being hit in the vicinity of the bride and groom, I can't help but follow them any more than a coffee addict can walk past a Starbucks.

Balls don't even have to be flying through the air or rolling onto greens for me to be distracted. The presence of the course, the mere *suggestion* of golf, is enough. I could tell you about the great bump-and-run by the guy in the white Polo shirt at what's-his-name's wedding, the hilarious triple-flub by the no-socks guy at the nuptials of That Guy My Wife Knows From Work and The Bride With Way Too Much Mascara, and I can recount in detail the off-the-flagstick almost-bunker-save by the leftie who book-ended his shot with generous swigs of Coors Light at the wedding with the pot bunkers and tri-level green—but I couldn't tell you a thing about these weddings themselves.

There is one solution I can think of. With the invitation to any wedding at a golf course, I ought to be given a tee time, or at least the option of trading my chicken or fish dinner for a bucket at the range. I could be back in time for speeches without anyone noticing, unless I forget to remove my glove, visor, spikes or frustrated expression.

This suggestion, though it may sound self-serving, actually reflects a desire to properly pay tribute to the blessed unions I'm asked to witness. Allowed to satisfy the golf fix I'd be craving anyway, I could turn my focus directly to the wedding once the round is done, giving bride and groom the attention they deserve. I'd be able to comment glowingly on the wedding gown and bridesmaid dresses; to joke sincerely, instead of falsely, about how I'm going to have to take my tux shirt to the dry cleaners because of all that dancing I did; to rave about how the band's frontman sounded just like the lead singer from Kool and the Gang when it performed "Celebration."

I'd be a valued wedding guest again. That's all I want. So if you're about to be married and decide that I count among your two or three hundred closest friends, please be sympathetic. Choose a nice church, synagogue, mosque or banquet hall instead of that beautiful golf and country club. Not only will I be thrilled to attend, I'll be able to tell you exactly how many roses were in the bridal bouquet. I'll gush about the excellence of the hors d'oeuvres. I'll tell you what everyone at my table does for a living, eats for breakfast and wears to bed. I'll be so present, the videographer will be lucky to get footage of anyone else. I'll be the guy who leads the conga line, the one who thanks your parents, the one who takes you aside during the reception to tell you it's been unforgettable.

Just don't do it with fairways, sand traps and water hazards as your backdrop. I'll be lucky to remember your names. But it's nothing personal.

Golfing with Steph

If you find yourself frustrated by golf—and odds are you do, since very few people and golf actually get along—I have a suggestion: Play a round, or at least hit a pail, with my wife.

I'm serious. She'll manage to make you feel good about your shots no matter what kind of bizarre trajectory they might take. One Saturday morning a while back, she insisted we go to the driving range together, which was by itself a wonderful gesture, since I know for a fact she has no more interest in golf than I have in shoe shopping.

Never mind how adorable she looked wearing a golf glove on her child-sized hand. Even more endearing was the fact that she found it a logical move to ask me how she should swing. I demonstrated a few, curving each ball 75 yards or so left, which astonished her. "How do you do that?" she said, eyes lighting up. No one had ever made me feel good about my slice before.

"I love you," I said.

"I'm serious, how do you do that? I want to do it."

"No you don't," I said. I tried to explain to her the elements of a good golf swing while telling her which parts of mine to ignore (all of them). She practised bringing the club up and back in super slo-mo and sweeping it back down in regular slo-mo, punching balls here and there, hitting some, missing others. Mostly she was really cute. She might not be pleased at my telling you this. She'd want me to say I was astounded at how naturally she displayed athletic flair, pounding the ball down the middle right away. But the truth is she was extremely cute.

With each few yards gained, she rejoiced. In the process, she made me feel like I was teaching her how to play golf. Now you have to think about this properly. I stink at golf. She made me feel like I was teaching it. Hence, I love her.

She told me she wanted to hit the 100 sign before we finished the pail. This was a difficult moment for me, not too far removed from "Do I look fat in these jeans?", since she hadn't hit a ball much farther than half that distance. There were maybe four balls remaining. I didn't say anything, which was dumb. Not saying anything is *always* the last option, yet it's the one we men usually choose. Frankly, I don't know how anyone can deal with us.

She topped one, then flew the second to maybe 75 yards. The third she hit 80. I was so proud of her, and, as I may have mentioned, she looked very cute. She lined up the last ball, brought the club back for ten minutes or so, then swept it back down. And you know what? The ball struck that 100 sign right in the middle of the first zero. I shouted, raised my arms, did the fist-pump, the whole ridiculous guy thing. She grinned and flipped the club aside. That wasn't just cute but pretty sexy, too.

If she can't make you feel good about your game, she'll at least distract you from it. You see, Stephanie loves to talk. If she's awake, she's talking. It's the first thing that made me fall for her. Okay, not the first thing. First thing was the body. But second was the great conversation. Now, I admit, when I first met her, and we talked for six or thirteen or a hundred hours straight or whatever it was, I assumed she was doing it to let me know she was interested. I didn't realize she actually just talks all the time.

And I'll tell you something. On the golf course, this is exactly what you want in a partner, as long as that partner isn't one of your normal buddies. If you're playing one of your usual terrible rounds and one of your regular playing partners can't stop nattering on about how you'll turn it around eventually, you mostly want to kill him. But Stephanie talks about other things, things that have nothing to do with golf. It doesn't matter if you're hitting or she's hitting or someone else is trying to line up a potential eagle putt. She'll be at address, and you think she's thinking about how to swing properly, but then, without lifting her head, she'll say something like, "Why do you think we didn't like *Good Will Hunting* even though everyone else did? Were we just not in the mood to like it?" or maybe "Let's have a wine-and-cheese party next Saturday night" or "Which one of my friends do you think is the prettiest?"

We played a nine-hole course a couple of summers ago, and she talked the entire time. You're thinking I must be kidding you, because it's impossible for someone to talk through nine straight holes of golf. But it's not impossible. I was there.

And here's the thing. While I experienced a few moments of frustration, for the most part I was just kind of loose and relaxed. I'll be honest, I can't always say that after a golf round. Okay, never. But she somehow kept me focused on other stuff.

By the way, she was right—we did like *Good Will Hunting* more the second time.

The Giant and the Devil

Sitting in the back of his brother-in-law Josh's jeep, listening to the Red Hot Chili Peppers' *Californication* and pretending to enjoy it (even though they've already said, "Sorry, Skeeter, you probably won't like this"), I spread my arms, stretch out my legs and lay my head back, happy for Kuz. It's a crisp autumn day. We're heading out of the city. And I'm going to play two world-class golf courses over the next two days. If one is to believe the hype, Le Géant and Le Diable are even more malevolent than their names imply. But golf course reviewers get paid for hyperbole; I'm sure they're no tougher than any number of courses I've played.

Eyelids drooping, I recall the only other time I visited Tremblant: a family ski trip perhaps a dozen years ago, when we never did end up skiing because the temperature at the peak of the mountain was minus 53, aided by skin-peeling winds that tore one of the T-bar lifts clear from the hill.

Nonetheless, as the urban landscape slowly gives way to mountains, I'm bathed by feelings of warmth and sweetness. For it was the Laurentians that had provided, five years earlier, the backdrop for the most pivotal moment of my life.

I'd arrived at the party in Montreal having told my friend Ira we were under no circumstances staying longer than the time it took to get the key from Jodi, the friend at whose apartment we were crashing. Ira, equally sapped from the Friday drive, hadn't argued.

We'd walked into the apartment, greeted Jodi, exchanged pleasantries with a handful of her friends and lingered at the door. I'd kept my chin down, trying to remain as invisible as possible.

Then I saw her, standing out by not trying to. Black pants, white top, irresistible midriff. I'd murmured to Ira, "We're staying."

Minutes later, she and I were sitting in opposite chairs leaning toward each other and trying to talk over the music. That conversation led to the one in the kitchen. The conversation in the kitchen became the one back at her friend Cheryl's apartment, Cheryl and Ira having taken a shine to each other, or at least having consented to pretend for our benefit. Though Stephanie and I talked uninterruptedly for several hours, I'd needed only the first five minutes to know I had never met a woman like this.

I observe Kuz as he sings along with the Chili Peppers, content to the degree only a man whose stag is looming can be content. I'm thrilled he and Francine have finally made it. Dan and Fran. Danny and Frannie. Kuzmarov and Gerstein. I know I'll be telling the story of my hand in this union multiple times over the next 48 hours, but I'm happy to tell it as many times as asked. After you've found the woman of your dreams, the next most gratifying thing you can do is help a friend find his.

When Stephanie and I decided to set up Kuz—my baseball friend and frequent companion on drives to Montreal—and Francine—Steph's former university roommate, same last name, no relation—our combined instinct was strong. There was no way these two wouldn't get along—both sweet, neither pretentious, well matched on the looks scale, shared musical vibe. We saw nothing but promise.

As we head deeper into the Laurentians and breathtaking yellows and oranges and crimson reds emerge, I remember how cocky Steph and I felt when the impossibly great first date bore out our hunch. Josh turns off the highway toward the main road leading to Tremblant as I recall grinning at Steph across the kitchen of our apartment—she on the phone with Frannie, receiving the report from one side, I on the cell phone with Kuz, receiving it from the other. They'd gone for dinner, walked a while, talked a while, gone back to his apartment, broken out the guitar, sung together until three in the morning. And so it went, nearly every day for three weeks, at the end of which, while throwing a ball back and forth one evening, Kuz said to me, "Skeeter, I'm crazy about Francine. I think she could be the one."

The Chili Peppers fade as Josh turns another corner and heads toward the main complex—Tremblant's hub, a European-style village of multi-colored chalets. As our cabin comes into view, half a dozen of Kuz's friends come out to greet him. The stag has officially begun.

In the first few minutes, introductions are made and roles cast. There's Steve, the Best Man; Josh, the Brother-in-Law and the Guy Guaranteed to Spend the Longest on His Hair; Jeremy, the Younger Brother, to be teased affectionately but looked out for; Rob, Organizer of the Weekend; Dave Brown, Kuz's Friend from Calgary, and the guy everybody likes because he's the worst golfer of the bunch but the best drinker; Sean and Shawn, odds-on Favorites to Shoot the Lowest Scores, and the guys whose high caliber of play will be implied by their coordinated golf outfits and numerous accessories; and me, regarded perhaps as the New Friend, or That Writer Guy Kuz Hangs Out With.

As we crack the tabs on some beers and initiate the bonding process by trading barbs at Kuz's expense *("Kuz is the only guy I know who showers four times a day"; "Kuz went to law school just long enough to decide he hated law"; "What do you figure Kuz weighs? A buck-fifty soaking wet?")*, I remember the phone call.

"Skeeter, it's over between me and Francine."

"Huh?"

"She said she just wants to be friends."

I remember his forlorn tone, his windless voice. I remember having dinner with him the next day, how inept I felt, how I said all the wrong things at the wrong times, how I didn't know whether to buck him up or tell him to move on. I was still convinced they were a match.

After an evening out, we snatch an hour or two of sleep and then, in early morning, make our bleary-eyed way to Le Géant. We warm up at the massive driving and chipping range, a rectangle of land so huge it feels like a missile testing ground. Josh, standing in one of the practice bunkers whose sand is so soft it feels like I'm on a Hawaiian shore, challenges me to a chipping contest. We spank balls out of the sand one after the other, then, having declared the contest a draw, move on to the range itself, where we take turns aiming for a flag 150 yards away.

Eyes starting to open fully, hangovers starting to lift, we drive our carts back to the first tee and receive a brief seminar from the starter, a peppy guy with a thick French accent who assures us that, no matter how well we play today, we will be out there no fewer than five hours. No problem, we all agree. A course this nice, a day this fine? Five hours, six hours—it's all good.

Well, not all good. Since I've got the unfortunate distinction of playing with the groom, my quartet is slated to kick things off. Kuz, Josh, Dave and I stand in a diamond and flip a tee in the air to see who will hit first. I know beyond any doubt, before the tee hits its apex, pauses and reverses direction, that it will be pointing toward me when it lands.

I push a tee into the ground feeling more anxious than on the day I proposed. I get into address, start the driver back and whip it through the zone. The heel of my club grazes the ball, sending it across my body and into a few small bushes that probably say to themselves, as the ball rolls into their dark undergrowth, *Hey, since when do balls ever come this way?*

I'm mortified, and more than a bit angry with myself—but the weekend's about Kuz, not me.

"And that's how it's done, boys," I say, breaking the tension and eliciting the first collective laugh of the day, which in any case earns one more credibility than playing 18 holes of solid golf.

As we crawl through the front nine, I realize why the practice range was so expansive. It was a harbinger of things to come. Everything about Le Géant is, well, giant. The combination of elevated tees, panoramic vistas and narrow, plunging fairways create a sense of immensity. That many of the holes require blind shots make the dimensions even more unsettling, as though you're wandering into one dimly lit room after another, fumbling for the light. After a few holes, I'm skeptical I'll manage even a bogey today.

Thankfully, it seems Dave might not manage a triple-bogey. If he isn't the worst golfer in history, he's close, which eases the pressure on me. Less pressure doesn't translate into better performance, of course, but at least I'm assured that, when the most offensive games are discussed over dinner tonight, my slice will have stiff competition from Dave's hook.

At the turn we pause for sandwiches and drinks, exchanging laughs over our front-half misadventures and teasing Kuz for his ridiculously intricate pre-shot routine. As I observe the bright smile on his face, the distinct expression of a man being ribbed by his friends, I recall the other phone call, more than two years after the first.

Following the three-week whirlwind and inexplicable break-up, Kuz and Francine had both moved on, dated others, started careers. And then, one evening, as I was hanging a picture on our apartment wall, Steph received a call from Frannie saying she'd been thinking lately—thinking about the guys she'd gone out with over the past while, and about how none of them, though they all had certain things going for them, measured up. Measured up to whom? asked Steph. Oh, no one in particular, said Frannie—though Daniel, in particular, had been especially nice. What was he up to these days, anyway?

When I called Kuz later that evening, I hoped he hadn't met anyone since we'd last spoken. I smile, remembering the way he tried to act cool when I mentioned Frannie's interest in going out again, the way he couldn't mask his excitement, the shared laugh Steph and I had about Frannie asking that we don't make her sound too eager when we speak to Daniel and Dan asking that we don't sound too eager when we relay his interest to Frannie.

The back nine continues pulling us along on an adventure of heart-stopping beauty and, at least as far as my round goes, mind-boggling ineptitude. From the split-level plateaus carved out of the mountainside we pause at length to appreciate the striking, paint-dipped views. On several holes we hit down-hill drives followed by uphill approaches, the kind of constant changes in elevation that may be fun on a roller coaster but that, on a golf course, get me quite grouchy.

At the eleventh, we stand atop a high tee box taking in the gorgeous vista of Tremblant's ski hill, silent now but soon to be teeming with flush-cheeked humanity. The hole is a 90-degree left-to-right dogleg, tempting righties to pound one around the corner for a possible birdie try. The two righties in our group, Josh and Dave, give it their best, but Josh misfires, overshooting the fairway instead, and Dave barely makes contact, reaching a spot closer to the ladies' tees than the fairway. Kuz and I, lefties, are happy not to be influenced by the temptation, content just to hit our balls straight and then deal with the rest of the hole as it's mapped out. This doesn't stop me from shanking two balls in the fairway and missing two putts, but at least I've still played the hole textbook. It's just that some of the pages are stuck together.

Befitting its name, the course is swallowing us whole, like a woman whose repeated abuse one can't help keep returning to be-cause she's just so damned good-looking. If the other foursomes are anything like us, I hope they brought plenty of extra sleeves.

Struggles aside, Kuz remains a picture of happiness. I think about the way he and Francine eased back in, how his certainty that they were born for each other must have battled fiercely against his desire not to get stung a second time. When the engagement was announced, Steph and I felt both validation and relief, agreeing to quit the matchmaking business while we were on top.

The eighteenth at Le Géant is considered by many the top par 4 in Canada. Standing on the tee and observing the steep descent toward the fairway, I'm thinking the tag might be changed to Hole Most Likely to Cause a Coronary. I make my way through the hole the way I have most others—slowly, crookedly and with a good number more strokes than the scorecard believes are necessary.

Removing my ball from the hole after putting out, I wonder whether the devil will be another form of the giant, whether I'll be able to apply the lessons from today when we head out tomorrow.

After another brief sleep and a shared bucket at, this time, a normal-sized range, I get my answer. Le Diable is not so much devilish as an exercise in outright sadism.

I don't need the pitiless 600-yard fifth hole to confirm this view. It's clearly established on the first two holes, both featuring massive waste bunkers lining the left side of the fairway.

I have two concurrent thoughts as we inch our way through the first and second. First, Le Diable may well be the most beautiful golf course I've ever played. Second, whoever named waste bunkers named them well. Coming upon your ball that has accidentally found its way into one, you feel scarcely more valuable than the pieces of debris among which it lies. In a regular sand bunker, one at least derives the pleasant association of beaches, warmth, the ocean. In a waste bunker, the sensation is of hitting off a slab of concrete covered with dirt, pebbles, twigs and other assorted litter.

The waste bunkers wind their way throughout Le Diable—on some holes, there are more acres of bunker than grass—which carves its impression upon you like a person whose unique features make her unforgettable even among other, more conventionally attractive, types. The fiery red sand traps suggest that an accidental slip in one of them might cause you to plunge through an actual portal to hell. Towering red pines create the sense of a medieval forest (though any aspiring dragon slayer would have to be much more effective with a sword than I am with a wedge).

I fare worse at Le Diable than I did at Le Géant by a few strokes. This only makes sense. A giant will simply outmatch you in size, but a devil takes multiple forms, disguises itself with outward beauty and persuades you to do things you know are mad.

We use our last few hours to enjoy some drinks in the village and take a few dozen final potshots at Kuz. Returning to the cabin, we pack our bags for a dawn departure. Kuz has confronted the giant and tangled with the devil. Now it's time to deliver him to his angel.

Lob Wedge or Hand Shears?

I pull into Andrew's driveway buzzing. Our tee time less than an hour away, I am already envisioning an exquisite opening shot and precise approach that will position me to begin the round with, in all likelihood, a bird, perhaps even an eagle.

"One minute," Andrew says, kneeling in the soil in front of his house. "Need to trim a couple of the rowdier branches." A few snips later, he steps back from the garden, deposits the ill-fated branches into a nifty little canvas sack, unstraps his Velcro knee pads and says, "Now, then. Let's go try to break a hundred for the thousandth time."

Sadly, the round goes as normal. Andrew and I, along with Rob and Dave, perform in typical fashion, that is, as though we have minimal vision, negligible dexterity and as much common sense as a lemming. Our practice strokes are unfailingly smooth and unhurried; our real ones, unfailingly graceless and panicked. It is as if, at the top of each backswing, some evil golf overlord flips a switch draining us of all coordination, then cackles, *Gotcha—again!*

Of course, the worse we play, the more we press, pushing our games further toward the brink of utter repugnance. By the last few holes we resemble crazed, khaki-clad inmates driven by an uncontainable desire to murder golf balls.

That is, three of us do. While Rob, Dave and I are gradually overtaken by the kind of self-possession displayed by the average infant, Andrew, as though not noticing the hideousness of his own game, strolls from shot to shot as unbothered as a polar bear. As we head sideways from the tee at 16 to search for our wayward drives, he as happy as if he'd just driven the green, I ask him whether he failed to notice his last shot—or the hundred before that.

"Just imagining myself in the garden," he says.

During the hour of post-round banter and beer, I feel that unique how-I-would-love-to-wrap-this-club-around-my-own-neck rage slowly recede. By the time I drop Andrew back at his house, it has ebbed almost fully, but still rears its head every few minutes to remind me of a particular flubbed chip, skidded putt or humiliatingly comical tee shot.

After shoving my clubs in the garage—and apologizing again for blaming them when I know it's really me—I pause in front of our garden, a parched rectangle about the size of a junior prison cell, and think of Andrew's absurd calmness.

I flip through the phone book and find an ad for a gardening center called Sheridan Nursery. I pay a visit—having no idea why it's called a nursery; I expect to see teams of nurses changing diapers and giving bottles—to investigate the spell that has settled over my oldest friend and long-time playing partner, who should by every right be prone to the same childish tantrums as the rest of us.

A disarmingly cheerful man dressed in earth tones offers his assistance. I ask to see some impatients, a type of flower I think I heard Andrew mention while I was pretending to listen to him.

"Actually, it's *impatiens*," says the man.

"That's what I said—impatients."

"Remove the t."

"There are two t's."

"Remove the one at the end."

A short time later I'm carting home two plastic trays of purple, pink and white impatiens lined up like little soldiers enlisted to distract the enemy by being pretty. The gardening guide I've bought tells me to quarter their undersides with two intersecting slices, enabling the roots to loosen. With my paring knife I delicately slice into the first impatien, which crumbles instantly. Instead of quartering it, I have millioned it.

Handling the next one like an egg, I perform the quartering successfully. Like sinking a two-foot putt, accomplishing one basic feat gives me the false impression I can do everything else. But, glancing back at the guide, I see I was supposed to add water to the hole first. Becoming impatient with the impatien, I start again, happy at least that I get to use my brand new extra-long-spout watering can.

Both trays emptied—two dozen impatiens in all—I stand and assess my work. While it's a safe bet no photographers from *Home & Garden* will be calling, this tricolor splash of vegetation gives me an undeniable lift. Is it the instinctive connection between man and nature? Our inherent desire to create beauty and order? The pleasant discovery that I've broken a sweat? Or just the temporary diversion from the golf-induced anger that only an hour ago had me wanting to punch out everyone on the planet?

The following Saturday, Andrew, Rob, Dave and I are at it again. The sky is overcast, yet I seem not to mind. I feel oddly centered, unperturbed even by Rob and Dave's apparent competition to see who can come up with the most obscure expletive to describe the playing conditions.

Though my game, as always, resembles that of someone who has just learned he has opposable thumbs, I feel different inside. The golf course is just a big, long, rolling garden. The trills of the birds, the honks of the geese, the drone of the crickets all seem enjoyable instead of distracting. The sand and water strike me as congruous elements of nature rather than malevolent ball-traps frothing at the mouth.

Tallying scores at the end of the round, I find I've carded 107—two strokes better than my previous effort. As Rob taunts Dave about his compulsion to take precisely five warm-up half-swings before every shot and Dave teases back about the fact that Rob looks like a robot with indigestion when he tees off, Andrew gives me a knowing smile.

I return to Sheridan Nursery, telling the cheery consultant I have mastered impatiens and am ready for the next level. He sketches a proposed layout for my garden more intricate than a molecular-biology diagram. "Don't be intimidated," he says, perhaps noticing my flop sweat. "It's easier than it looks."

He also suggests a few additional implements I should purchase. As helpless in the face of garden accessories as I am before a display of Pinnacle Golds at 20 percent off, I come home with a fork, spade, hoe, garden rake, yard rake, regular hand shears, industrial-strength hand shears and something called a cultivator that looks like an early-pitchfork reject. Stephanie comes outside to see me turning soil amid a pile of tools and asks what I'm doing.

"Improving my golf game," I reply. "Got you something." I present the lavender gardening gloves I've bought her, complementing my black pair.

"I had no idea you were into gardening."

"Love, I'm into anything that might help me break a hundred."

The next weekend Andrew, Rob, Dave and I decide to tackle a new course. Again I am infused by an unexpected equanimity. Even after my first tee shot—a ball that immediately swerves away in search of its home planet—my feeling of quietude prevails, whereas this kind of shot usually threatens to detonate my brain. After hitting a drive twice as ugly as mine, Andrew says, "Well, that hardly went as planned. Unfortunate." Rob and Dave look at him suspiciously.

Rob, after nailing a drive whose hook matches my slice, immediately snaps, turning the color of eggplant while swearing at his club for two uninterrupted minutes. Dave says, "Watch me crush this one," then sends a divot the size of a good-sized pancake about 30 feet and the ball about half that distance. He murmurs an expletive, looks to the sky with the expression common to all duffers, the one that asks God for the shot back, and then, when God stays mum, smashes his club against the ground and curses his mother for giving birth to him.

While my game is hardly impressive—and by hardly impressive I mean completely laughable—the strokes I usually waste out of frustration or rushing are not wasted, since I feel neither frustrated nor rushed. Saving those few critical strokes, I edge tantalizingly closer to the Holy Grail, finishing at 103. In the clubhouse Andrew and I exchange Zen-like grins as Rob ribs Dave about his uneven tan and Dave mocks Rob about the fact that when standing over a putt he looks like an octogenarian with gallstones.

Following the round I return to the nursery to purchase the specially designed knee pads I have been resisting. Though they serve approximately the same function as the hockey knee pads I already own, the stink from any part of my hockey equipment would annihilate all plant life within six miles, so I buy these instead. I also acquire a weeder for the dual reason that it looks easy to use and, when I ask Mr. Earth Tones if I need one, he smiles as though I've asked whether oxygen is necessary for breathing.

I go to bed finding I'm hoping for rain in the morning instead of sun, rain being better for the flowers. I anticipate having dreams about gardening nymphs polishing the petals of my impatiens or nightmares about rival goblins trying to make off with them. I switch to the Gardening Channel when Stephanie leaves the room and back to ESPN when she returns. "Why don't you keep it on the Gardening Channel?" she says.

"I don't watch the Gardening Channel."

"Of course you don't, honey. By the way, you fell asleep reading your *Guide to Perennials* again last night."

The next day, my fixation migrates from the garden to the front lawn. I spread several bags of manure and sprinkle grass seed over the bare patches as meticulously as if I were looking for land mines, minding little that the excess manure is cascading into the backs of my shoes. I nurture the new grass with greater care than that with which I raised my sons, watering twice a day, staring at the droplets glistening on the striving blades, telling them they can make it if they want to badly enough.

Over the course of the season, the two endeavors continue to push each other along. I struggle for a balanced golf game as zealously as I do a harmonious garden. I anticipate with equal pleasure a morning of mashing Top-Flites or an afternoon of yanking weeds. I repeat the same silly blunders on the links and in the soil, chiding myself for making them and then making them again.

Each pursuit earns both my respect and my willing obsession—because each is as unforgiving as it is exhilarating. Mess up an individual step and you see it in the overall result. Try to take shortcuts and the eventual goal only moves further away. Overcompensate for flaws instead of fixing them and the flaws only become more evident.

However, in both cases, when you get it right, the result—whether a pretty flower smiling up at you or a gorgeous ball dropping quietly onto the green—is a moment of beguiling beauty. And it takes only one such moment to hook you forever.

The Twenty-Three Dumbest Things You Can Say on a Golf Course

1. Dogleg, shmogleg—I'm going over those trees.

2. My friend told me that to get out of the sand you just aim an inch behind the ball and swing like hell.

3. Laying up is for wimps.

4. I think I got all the kinks out on the range.

5. Damned right I can carry the lake.

6. I always hit my 6-iron straight down the middle.

7. I'm pretty sure I can reach this in two.

8. I can't see over that hill, but I doubt there's anyone there.

9. I heard you should always aim right at the hazard you're trying to avoid.

10. Why don't we play from the golds?

11. I'd better not leave this one short.

12. That's it, I'm switching balls.

13. I made an adjustment to my swing the other day that should really make a difference.

14. Maybe it's in the cup.

15. Nice front nine, boss, but now I'm going to have to feed you to the sharks.

16. It doesn't look like there's any water up there. Time to break out the heavy lumber.

17. Is that an extra ball in your pocket, or are you just happy to see me?

18. Instead of punching out, I wonder if I can blast one between those two branches and then fade it back toward the hole.

19. I'll give you 50 bucks if you make that putt.

20. There's absolutely no way I should use a 3-wood here. Then again, what the hell.

21. I saw Tiger try this once.

22. Does anyone know how to get blood off a 9-iron?

23. Mark it down: this is the day I break 100.

Taking It to the Next Level

About the sport of golf today we know two things. First, the players are better—an inevitable trend in any sport. Each generation gets a little bigger, a little stronger. People in one era tend to take care of themselves more intelligently than those who came before. This is true of the current generation, unless you count crystal meth addictions, unchecked pollution and widespread obesity. The law of natural progress dictates that, as a species, over time we will achieve fractional increments of improvement, which is why we will one day witness someone run the 100-meter dash in three seconds flat.

Second, equipment is superior—far superior to that of even a decade ago. This is also unavoidable. The pace of technological advance means we shouldn't be surprised if, within a few years, a composite shaft consisting of Styrofoam, polypropylene, fiberglass and boron hits the market that increases average tour driving distance to 700 yards. Yes, the odd purist will continue to argue for persimmon clubs and against snug-fitting, dry-fit, pectoral-revealing Nike tops, but let's face it, you can't stop progress any more than you can hit a low 3-iron into a blind dogleg.

Accepting the dual advance of talent and technology, however, doesn't help address the serious issue facing the PGA today: fan indifference. Whether or not it's true, a good number of people feel golf was more interesting before Big Bertha drivers and martini-glass torsos, just as tennis was more interesting before oversized rackets and serves that burn up on reentry. Is it reasonable to say that when athletes get too good at a certain sport, or their equipment too sophisticated, the sport is doomed? Of course not. Sports that endure do so because they're inherently compelling: baseball because of its timelessness and magical dimensions; football for its combination of violence and grace; basketball because it's played at altitudes those of us with six-inch verticals can hardly fathom.

Golf seizes anyone who plays it because it satisfies two powerful human desires equally: The desire to experience nature and the desire to see if one can put a ball in a hole. Give a one-year-old the choice to play with a set of cards, build a tower of blocks or drop the same ball into the same cup for several minutes on end, and he'll choose the latter every time. Why? Because our instinct to play games is as strong as our instinct to build rockets that tell us whether Mars ever harbored life. It is for this reason that, when one Scot picked up a wooden stick so many centuries ago and tried to knock a pebble into a nearby hollow, he kicked off a chain reaction still on the ascent.

So, while golf isn't in danger, not really, it is getting somewhat stale. What can be done? Well, to influence how people react to a game, one has to change the nature of the game itself.

Making the courses more difficult would seem the most obvious solution, but designers have been going at it all wrong by adding length. If players are already hitting it longer, these architects figure, let's stretch out the courses, and the fans will be back on the edges of their seats in no time. In truth, lengthening courses is no different than raising basketball nets. Golfers are going to continue getting stronger just as basketball players are going to continue getting taller.

Fans would be more engaged by courses that impose a greater challenge. But if the powers that be are going to make the courses harder, I urge them to do it in earnest. I'm not talking about fairways 40 yards wide instead of 50. I'm talking about fairways ten yards wide. I'm talking about checkerboard fairways with alternating grass and sand squares from tee to green. I'm talking about 30-foot earth walls rising just beyond the tees, requiring true shotmaking.

To keep fans watching, new elements need to be constantly introduced to the game, and changing the way courses look or play can accomplish this little, since the most spectacular golf course on earth, after all, still resembles the least spectacular at its essence. The scenery *around* a golf course, however, can vary dramatically from place to place. Banff Springs scarcely resembles Royal Troon. The eighteenth at Pebble Beach hardly calls to mind the eleventh at Ballybunion. There are more golf courses being built all the time, but they're being built, by and large, in new corners of the same areas. The golf world needs to scout untapped areas and then give course designers free rein.

How about the Gobi Desert, for instance? The winds at St. Andrew's would be a walk in the park compared to a good old-fashioned desert sandstorm. Or some sub-zero conditions? These days, the pros look like they're about to die if it starts to drizzle and the temperature drops below 80. Let's toughen them up. A round at Carnoustie would pale in comparison to one at, say, Siberia National.

Only the imaginations of those at the top could limit the possibilities. Antarctica. Nunavut. The Australian Outback. The Bonneville Salt Flats. Muir Woods.

Or the Amazon Basin. Eighteen holes at Bethpage Black? Nothing compared to a tournament at Amazon Greens. Go out of bounds and you might be searching for your ball alongside a touchy boa constrictor. Now that's entertaining golf. (This has good practical implications, too. You want job creation? Know how many people it takes to build a course in the middle of the desert? Neither do I—but I bet it's a lot.)

The next step would be to take a critical look at today's rules—which, let's face it, are wimpy. I'm not suggesting an overhaul, just some slight modifications. Full-contact golf, for instance, or at least arm-wrestling matches to decide tie scores. Come to think of it, forget arm-wrestling. Why not a sudden-death format in which the first golfer to hit a hole-in-one wins the tournament? Playoff competitors, placed at a specific par 3, would alternate shots until one of them scores the ace, no matter how long it takes. With every shot, galleries would become more frenzied, their giddiness growing with every miss, their collective tremor rising with each ball that just skirts the flag. Imagine the buzz after 50 shots, 60, 100. Gallery members would take turns sprinting to the concession stand, praying they weren't missing the ace during their turn in line. Those watching from home would stay tuned in not only to witness the eventual winner but also to see how long those in the gallery stick around. The playoff might last hours, or even days, which would make for supreme theater and provide unforgettable stories for those in attendance. *I missed my tenth anniversary, my daughter's Thanksgiving pageant and the Queen's visit—but I was there for Tiger's Ninth-Hour Ace.*

Here's another idea: Any caddy is allowed to kidnap and impersonate his counterpart, causing his real partner's rival to wonder why he keeps hitting pitching wedges that he believes ought to have been 2-irons. And another: Allow the foot wedge or hand toss on designated holes. Since the urge to kick one's ball is always bubbling at the surface, why not allow the choice? Twice per nine holes, one may kick his ball instead of striking it with the golf club. An additional two times, he may throw or roll it. Now we're getting somewhere.

Finally, let's look to other popular sports for suggestions, since there must be a reason they're adored by so many (other than croquet—that one's tough to figure out). Golf has always existed in a kind of proud self-containment, but it can learn about how to win fans by looking beyond its own country club universe to other sporting bodies—in particular the enterprise whose track record leaves all others in the dust.

I'm referring, of course, to the World Wrestling Federation—or maybe it's called the World Wrestling Association these days, or the Wrestling League of America, or the Corporeal Thespians Guild. While I'm not a fan of the sport (and by sport I mean joke), one can't deny it as a model of fan loyalty.

Wrestling's secrets aren't secrets at all. In fact, they're similar to writers' secrets, and just as obvious. Create memorable characters, place them in conflict, make them behave consistently, though not always predictably, and offer entertaining resolutions that at the same time cause people to consider the great moral and philosophical questions of our existence.

Okay, maybe not that last point. But wrestling certainly has the thing about characters and conflict down. So why not spice up the PGA Tour similarly? The largest clash we've been offered in recent memory involved Fuzzy Zoeller suggesting Tiger had a bias toward fried chicken and collard greens. I didn't see anyone buying extra tickets to see if the two might drop the gloves (that is, carefully unsnap the gloves, then remove each finger one by one) and go toe to toe. Then there was the decision by Hal Sutton to pair Tiger and Phil Mickelson at the 2004 Ryder Cup despite the possibility that *they might not like each other*. Not exactly the stuff of great drama. Fodder for a primetime soap, perhaps, but not good enough for today's sports fan, who can just as easily switch to the X Games to get his adrenaline fix.

Let's start by borrowing wrestling's most basic element: cool nicknames. Sure, the mention of Arnie's Army still awakens something inside us, and Golden Bear just might be the best moniker in sports. But today's golfers, through no fault of their own, are largely a bland, interchangeable group, the most attention-seeking of them reduced to wearing extremely ugly outfits because they can't think of any other way to get noticed, besides winning, which I can tell you from experience is sometimes exceedingly hard to do.

I suggest the PGA come up with a list of new nicknames and circulate them to the top 50 golfers on tour, who may then choose on a first-come, first-served basis. Golf commentators, their creativity currently restricted by having to murmur remarks like "That's a nice golf shot" or "Still not comfortable, he's checking out the slope from the opposite side of the hole a third time," would seize the opportunity to spout more engaging messages.

Ernie the Eviscerator is clinging to a slim lead with Chainsaw Weir and R-Goose not far behind.

And, as with wrestling, why not add an element of true physical confrontation? Someone's about to putt when he gets a low-voltage shock from his playing partner, whose caddy distracted the other caddy for a few critical moments, turning the match. *Jumbo did not see that coming! Phil the Furious brilliantly sneaked his way into the gallery, blended in, then buzzed him right in the hammy just as his putter was starting back. Jumbo is sprawled on the green, folks, and you know he'll be that way for at least the next ten minutes!*

Give players the opportunity to execute a maximum of three Hostile Maneuvers per match to help close scoring gaps. These moves would have to be planned carefully and used judiciously. When it's late in the day and a player is down two strokes, wouldn't it be great if he were allowed one crowbar-like swat at the back of his playing partner's knees? Viewers would sit on the edges of their seats as the player, walking down the fairway at 15, removes the crowbar only to have his caddy advise him to save it for later in the match.

Wrestling isn't the only sport from which positive elements might be borrowed. From football, golfers might discover a greater flair for playing to the crowd, developing signature dances to punctuate key putts. From basketball players they could learn the rhythms and vocabulary of trash talk, so that we might hear Fred Couples bellow to Jim Furyk before a critical approach, "JF dawg, yo' mama's so ugly she slapped you when you came out. That's what I'm talkin' about."

Even features of miniature golf could spice up the parent game. How about a vertical log swinging back and forth an inch above the cup on a critical tournament hole? Or a true blending of the large-scale sport with its diminutive version: Separate every two regulation-sized holes with a miniature one, with the best combined score winning on Sunday.

I appreciate that a sport can't be changed overnight, and I'm hardly suggesting the PGA ought to implement all of my ideas at once. It might make better sense to implement them over two or three seasons. In fact, it's a good bet you're wondering why I haven't been asked to join the PGA's Governing Body or Advisory Council. The answer is: I don't know. But if, within a few years, you happen to be flipping channels and come upon a sudden-death hole-in-one competition to decide a major, don't say I didn't warn you. You can thank me later.

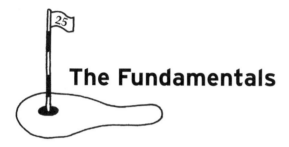

The Fundamentals

In no sport can you do the spectacular without first mastering the basics. You can't perform a reverse dunk without knowing how to do a simple lay-up. You can't hit a running forehand down the line before learning a garden-variety groundstroke. You can't turn a slick double-play unless you know how to catch and throw the ball in the first place. You can't land a triple axel until you know how to ... okay, you probably won't ever land a triple axel.

The fundamentals are more important in golf than in any other sport (except perhaps checkers, which sports purists may argue is not a true athletic pursuit). Golf requires the simultaneous execution of three zillion tiny movements to create one fluid swing, and if even seven of those three zillion parts are missing, that fluid swing turns into something more like a piece of scrap metal being swung by a robot whose circuitry is failing.

I am, it must be said, a poor golfer. Put another way, I suck the bag. However, I do have a firm grasp of the rudiments, despite my inability to apply them once actually standing on a golf course. I'm like a student who understands the concepts behind basic arithmetic but can't figure out how to use an abacus. But there's no reason you shouldn't benefit from my knowledge.

There are only a handful of basic skills one needs to play golf well. The first one any golfer must learn is the one he will use the most often: lying. To lie effectively on a golf course is not as easy as it may look, especially to the novice whose dignity still matters to him. In the first place, lying must be done selectively. If you usually shoot over 100 and then suddenly report six birdies in a row, chances are your playing partners are going to get suspicious. But the occasional par declared in place of a double-bogey will slip through with barely a notice. The instinct may be harder to control than you think, since lying on a golf course (not to be confused with reclining on a golf course) is addictive for two reasons: It's naughty, and it makes us seem better than we are.

Just as you shouldn't lie too often, you shouldn't lie too big. No one's going to believe the fisherman who says he caught a six-ton pickerel, and no one's going to believe your claim that you shot 17-under last week at your home course where you usually card 17 on the first three holes.

A series of small lies will, in the end, help your game more than a few implausible ones because, while people will generally let slide any number of small fibs, their consciences will insist they speak up when a playing partner declares he just birdied a hole in which they saw him take three shots just to get out of the greenside trap. I recently played with a guy who never gave himself higher than double on a given hole. He said this was because of his handicap. This is a prime example of a ridiculous lie, since it should be clear to anyone with a few functioning brain cells that, if you have to change your score to preserve your handicap, you're lying about your handicap. If, on the other hand, this liar had scored himself normally, claimed later that he'd had a bad day, and still walked around declaring the handicap he so desperately wanted to retain, I wouldn't have thought twice about it. We all have bad days on the course. Actually, they're the only kind of days I have.

Related to lying, but essential on its own, is the ability to make excuses. Any golfer who doesn't have this in his arsenal had better be able to shoot 90 blindfolded, or at least hog-tied. Otherwise, he needs to learn how to plant the right excuse at the right time.

It's important to start with simple, straightforward excuses before getting cute. If you've never practised how and when to mention a sore shoulder or sprained ankle prior to tee-off, don't start playing around with more elaborate alibis. Before you start talking meningitis, try dropping subtle mention of a hairline pinkie fracture instead; before you throw around stomach flu or The Worst Headache in History, try something simpler, like a bruised thumb. A golf excuse needs to satisfy only two criteria to work: it should be believable, and impossible to disprove.

More important, don't wait until the round has begun to start making excuses; do it ahead of time. No matter how subtly you rationalize your abysmal play during the round, unless you've planted the seed beforehand, it will come off as the pathetic attempt to save face it actually is. Blurting, "My shoulder is absolutely killing me!" one trillisecond after you muff your initial drive doesn't hold any water unless, over breakfast before the round, you grabbed your shoulder at least once while buttering your muffin.

It is important to note that those who get the most mileage out of their excuses are the ones who play them down. After you've demonstrated that the effort of muffin-buttering has caused that twinge in your shoulder to flare up, and your friend Gary says, "Shoulder hurting, man?" don't respond by saying, "Lord, yes— it's like there's a set of freaking steak knives in there." Tell him, "It's nothing, Gare. Strained it doing an extra set of incline presses yesterday." If you mention your injury every other hole and act desperate for others to acknowledge how debilitating it is, the people around you will wish you'd stayed home. But if you subtly wince when you pull the bathroom door open or suddenly grab the back of your knee while walking out of the pro shop, you'll automatically be forgiven at least half a dozen bad shots.

Another critical skill to master in golf is that of replacing your divots. After taking a swath out of the ground the size of an elephant's tongue, the average golfer, if he undertakes the eight-foot walk to retrieve his divot in the first place, will angrily throw it back down in the general vicinity of its original home before muttering an expletive, hitting his bag and moving on. But the complete golfer takes time and care, aligning the divot's edges against the original contour and tamping it down slightly before muttering an expletive, hitting his bag and moving on.

There is some question as to how large a divot needs to be to demand replacing. Here's a good rule of thumb: Replace your divots. As an alternative, you can choose never to play anywhere but in South Florida, where all you have to do, no matter how big a chunk you take from the ground, is take a scoop of sand from your cart and pour some into the hole you've made. It's like a portable toy sandbox. Many people believe South Florida is a preferred golf destination for its flawless climate, stunning courses and crushed-ice piña coladas, when in fact the reason is that you can pour sand into your divots instead of having to find the offending piece of grass and replace it, which, after all, only reminds you how bad your shot was. Put another way, South Florida not only takes the pressure off you to find and replace your divots, it lets you play with a plastic scoop throughout the round, too.

The next skill of importance to the beginning golfer is ball moving. This skill can take a bit more time to master. The novice ball mover tips his hand by a) rushing ahead to get to his ball before anyone else and b) looking extra innocently at his playing partners as he stands over his ball, meaning he is in the process of moving it with his foot. Like cheating any system, you're only going to be successful if you act as though nothing is unusual. Proceed to your ball with the others, approach it as though you're not bothered by the fact that it's four feet into the rough, and relax. Bend over to move a leaf or twig near the ball and kick it to the desired location in one movement. You'll only have a moment in which to do this. Keep the others in your peripheral vision, pretend you're deciding which club to select, and then, the moment they turn away, notice the leaf or twig.

The most ambitious of ball movers, once they've mastered the basic skill, may try ball planting. Good ball planters save several strokes each round by "finding" balls seemingly lost in the woods or at the edges of lakes. To be able to plant balls successfully, one must do three things. First, he must always have an extra ball in his pocket, since it will look obvious if he loses a ball, unzips a pocket of his bag then finds the one assumed to be lost. Second, he must ensure the ball in his pocket is the same make as the one he is currently using, since delightedly coming upon a Pinnacle you claim is yours, when someone in your group knows you were hitting a Top-Flite, will only reveal you as the cheat you are. Finally, the aspiring ball planter must find his balls (so to speak) no more than twice per round, and only when it is reasonable to believe the balls are findable. In other words, if your drive splashes into the middle of a lake in full view, and you then "find" it at the edge of the lake, you're just not cut out for cheating. Similarly, if your ball is seen entering the woods on a severe angle two-thirds of the way up a 100-foot tree, then you miraculously discover that it must have rattled around and kicked out onto the fairway, you deserve that penalty stroke and more. Choose your ball-planting moments for drives that may or may not have bounced into the woods or shots that roll over hills toward hidden creeks.

Finally, the average golfer is no golfer at all unless he learns how to loosen the strap of his playing partner's bag from the golf cart so that it falls with a crash as he drives away. A good golfer should be able to get away with this at least once per round; top recreational golfers can execute the trick up to four times. My friend Rob once got me half a dozen times in a single round. I maintained deep admiration for his mischief during the entire two weeks I didn't speak to him. Strap loosening may not make a difference to your own scorecard, but if it's done effectively it will make your playing partner increasingly angry—and everyone knows the true measure of a golfer is not whether he can raise his own game but whether he can cause others to play worse.

Putting My Game to the Test

For some time now, I've suspected that I'm a dismal golfer. Evidence ranges from three-putts more frequent than Royal Family splits to the fact that half of my drives end up in the next city.

Still, a part of me wants to blame the clubs I use, the courses I play or the irregularity with which I get out. So I decide to subject my game to rigorous scientific testing—five different courses, five different sets of clubs, on five separate days—to answer the question *Does poor golf transcend all other factors?*

In case I do prove the hypothesis, I want to take pleasure in the process, so I choose as my field lab the Palm Beach area of South Florida, where the worst grievance possible is that one might awaken on a given morning to find the temperature is 81 degrees instead of 83.

I begin at Emerald Dunes, one of the top-ranked public courses in the United States. My round begins with the lovely discovery that the trio with whom I am placed all hail from my hometown of Toronto. The round then takes an immediate downturn when I learn they are each club pros at courses I play with equal ineptitude. They inform me they will be playing from the golds. I tell them to enjoy themselves.

Emerald Dunes justifies its name with immaculate, bright green fairways that curl charmingly around ubiquitous water. Not only is the course appealing, but, as a bonus, carts are equipped with GPS yardage monitors, which would be a major benefit were I able to control my shots any better than a butterfly collector might control a pit bull.

The first several holes are characterized by lakes along the edge of the fairways that don't seem bothersome until my slice reminds me that it can bring virtually any element, no matter how seemingly irrelevant, into play. On the seventh, unsettled by the combination of a turtle sunning itself on a rock and a hawk floating overhead, I turn an eight-foot putt for bogey into a six-foot putt for double.

Nearing the turn, one of the pros suggests I try to align my body with the target. This seems too logical. I'm suspicious of him for the rest of the round.

At the eleventh, a dazzling elevated tee shared with 18, I send my ball veering into the drink. As usual, penalty strokes, combined with less short-game finesse than an orangutan, are killing me. By the end of the round I've sliced, shanked and flubbed my way to a 112. I imagine the club pros will spend the next few hours debating which was more amusing, my driving like an epileptic or my putting like a blind man.

The following day, I head to the PGA National Golf and Sports Club complex, which contains five separate 18-hole layouts: the Estate Course, the Champion, the Squire, the Haig and the General, the latter four named, respectively, for Nicklaus, Sarazen,

Hagen and Palmer. I'm placed on the General, so termed because one is supposed to tackle it as Arnie would. In fact, my scorecard reads, *Arnold Palmer attacked golf courses with unharnessed fury*, so we're actually not that different.

I'm placed with a husband-and-wife pair from Pittsburgh, Bill and Patty, a typical hacker and hackeresse. Bill sports a 1970s-style mustache and sunglasses at least 20 percent too wide. Patty returns my greeting then seems to go silent, mostly because she has difficulty getting a word in against Bill's constant patter. While we're waiting for the group ahead of us to advance, Bill takes the opportunity to inform me that Pittsburgh natives refer to Philadelphia as Filthydelphia. He seems to take pleasure in relating this information, as though he's just gone a point up on Filthydelphia in their ongoing battle.

As I observe the enormous sweep of the first hole, the starter tells us the course favors those who can play left to right. As a leftie whose slice makes planetary orbits look small, I consider this less-than-ideal news.

PGA's picturesque lakes, bridges and fountains make me feel as though I've jumped into a postcard. Not that any self-respecting golf postcard would allow me into it. By the time I arrive at the seventeenth—an elegant par 3 to a partial island green protected by a monstrous lake and bunkers at the rear; from the air it must look like a multi-eyed monster gobbling one golf ball after another—I'm already at the despised, but familiar, century mark. Bill and Patty haven't fared much better, Bill having spent most of the round saying things like "That wasn't bad, arm was nice and straight" to Patty after she punches each ball 50 yards straight ahead, though I suspect he really means, "Why don't you pick the damn thing up already?"

I manage bogey, then bogey again at 18, a spectacular par 5 meandering around a sparkling lake and toward a two-tiered green protected by more sand than an emergency flood center. I finish at 110.

Next is the Country Club course of the Boca Raton Resort Club. Untwisting my tongue after reciting the name to the hotel concierge, I shuttle-bus over, energized by a new day, a new round and new possibilities. My playing partners are a trio of pharmaceutical salesmen in town for a conference. I'm pleased to discover that their games are all as ugly as mine and their outfits even less coordinated.

Sadly, most of the new possibilities I create involve innovative ways to lose golf balls. Boca opens before me like a breathtaking woman revealing herself—but, like an unskilled lover, I'm all over the map. The round is exemplified by my exploit on the second hole, when, stretching out on my stomach to retrieve my ball at the edge of a pond, I inadvertently place my knee directly in a fire-ant hill, resulting in fantastic itching for the rest of the day and a kneecap that looks as though it has been dive-bombed by every mosquito in North America in a span of 30 seconds.

The handsome fairways at Boca are narrow but playable. That is, if one proceeds intelligently and with restraint, he'll do fine—which explains why I'm seven over after four holes. Flailing away with my driver as though it's a fire hose, unwilling to hit safe irons, or even slightly less safe 3-woods, off the tee, I place myself in one impossible position after another, amusing my playing partners to no end and making me want to take up a different game—marbles, perhaps—permanently.

I approach the lovely par-3 fifth. Miss left, and there's sand; miss right or long, water. At this point, what I miss is the safety of my cart. Before I get a chance to embarrass myself, Randall, one of the pharma gents, performs a near-impossible feat. After catching his drive well, he watches it slice right, right, right, then plug in the far bank of the lake. It's a comical image, that little white ball staring back at us from 200 yards away. Randall tees up another. He catches this one well, too. It starts straight but then begins fading right, right, right ... and plugs three inches to the left of the first ball. Now there are two eyes.

Coming off the turn, I find sand on three out of five holes (not the sand actually positioned to snare shots; the other sand, placed there merely for decoration). On 15 I learn that one of my playing partners is from the Canadian town of Timmins, birthplace of Shania Twain. Envisioning Shania, I lose what flickering bits of concentration I've been able to muster.

Ambling toward the eighteenth, I keep my scorecard in my pocket. The information it contains isn't positive, I know, so there's no need to detract from my appreciation of this course, which hugs the land so naturally it feels as though it emerged intact as the earth cooled. Eighteen is similar to many other holes at Boca, tempting me to skirt a long, curving lake or, with a herculean iron, carry it. Instead I go cautiously, coming away with par—and a final tally of 114—then head over to the beach, where I'm reminded how much I enjoy the image of sand when it doesn't include one of my golf balls.

The penultimate scene, three days later, is Delray Beach Golf Club, an agreeable public course tucked into a residential enclave. I'm paired with Joe from upstate New York, a sweaty barrel of a man whose first words are, "Had too much Canadian Club last night." I'd like to think he's making a Canuck reference for my benefit, but the powerful scent of rye coming from his pores changes my mind.

Joe's alcohol-soaked aroma, chain smoking and taut New York energy don't seem to affect me. At Delray Beach, everything comes together, and I am playing bogey golf—for two holes. My game, suddenly out of its element, seeks a more familiar zone. Delray's generally forgiving layout is offset by several sadistically positioned flags, many of which cost me strokes by convincing me to aim for them, resulting instead in sand visits, balls rolling off the backs of greens or chip shots from rough that hasn't been trimmed since Churchill's last cigar. I finish at 108.

My experiment concludes at The Breakers Ocean Course, the oldest 18-hole course in Florida, so beautifully maintained it seems as though a team of landscaping elves rush out of the clubhouse every night to snip each last blade of grass to identical height.

At just under 6,200 yards, Breakers is somewhat short—but director of golf Tim Collins, my partner for the round, warns me not to get cocky. Because the land around the stately Breakers Hotel has been maximized, virtually no room for error exists, and serious shotmaking is required.

Tim isn't kidding. Enjoying the stunning view of the hotel from the first green, I forget I've already taken five shots to get there. Made anxious by this realization, I take three more to finish the hole. My lack of focus persists throughout the round, and as a result I go through two sleeves of balls faster than you can say *double titanium*.

Coming into the final three holes, I'm carding 92. I have a decent shot at ducking under my four other scores. But Breakers's marvelous 16–17–18 sequence distracts me from the few positive swing elements I try to remember before each shot. On the gorgeous par-3 sixteenth, featuring a green the size of my thumbnail guarded by water on the right and sand on the left, I take triple-bogey. At 17, a sweet par-5 dogleg that makes one's trip to the green utterly enjoyable, if too long, I show off my legendary finishing skill by rolling my first putt well past the hole, then leaving my second short. Double.

Coming home on 18, an impeccable par 4 that whispers up to the foot of the clubhouse—to greet the elves, I suppose—I remember to align my body to the target. Unfortunately, I still have no choice but to use my own golf swing to hit the ball. My 9-iron approach scoots off the toe of the club and into what Tim informs me is native fakahatchee grass. I ask about other exotic flora on the course so that I can drop their names when describing the day to Stephanie to distract her from asking about the actual round.

I find the fakahatchee-surrounded ball and, after what seems like days, persuade it onto the green. A two-putt leaves me with another double, and an overall 110.

My five rounds go like this: 112, 110, 114, 108, 110. The unsightliness of my game now scientifically confirmed, I feel nonetheless that the experiment was a triumph, since it bore out the hypothesis that bad golf transcends variations in clubs, playing partners or frequency of play.

Thus enlightened, I recline in a beach chair, stare out at the waves and resolve to investigate a new line of research next season: the impact of lessons.

Everything I Needed to Know About Golf I Learned from My Toddler

My three-year-old, Julian, may still be behind me in a few areas—he can't handle my knuckleball, for instance—but when it comes to golf, the only six rules I need can be derived from him:

1. **Don't rush.** When Julian is figuring out how his toy phone works, he goes about it with uncanny patience. I could smash a pair of cymbals behind him and he wouldn't flinch. I try to reflect this self-possession whenever I'm facing a tough putt. I breathe, examine the slope, then lightly grasp the shaft—and usually sail the ball past the hole anyway. But the principle holds.

2. **Don't cheat.** While it's true cheating is one of the basic skills golfers learn almost instinctively—even the most moral of us has the occasional urge to use our foot wedge—this doesn't mean it's right to act on such an instinct. Whenever the wicked impulse ripples through me, I think of the way in which Julian

methodically works his way through every task without ever considering a shortcut. Or I just remind myself that the saved stroke will probably change a 113 to a 112, neither of which is likely to earn me that tour card.

3. **Tune out.** While a toddler's incredible focus can prove challenging in some contexts—say, when you're trying to get him to the table; or dressed; or to bed; or anywhere at any time under any circumstances—it serves as a great model for golf. If Julian is pushing a fire engine across the floor, nothing in the world exists but him and that fire engine. If I could develop the same kind of Zen-like relationship with a golf ball, it would doubtless be much kinder in return.

4. **Ignore obstacles.** If Julian sees a book he wants sitting across the room, he simply puts his head down and starts running, heedless of what might be in his way. If the sofa is in his target line, he'll bounce off it and keep going, always thinking of the ultimate target. I'd love to be able to maintain this perspective when coming to one of those tee-facing lakes that seem to metamorphose even as you address the ball. The adult brain is truly a hindrance.

5. **Swallow your pride.** Most of us reject advice about our games as fast as we cut off telemarketers. But it's hard to progress in any pursuit without sound guidance. Julian understands this. If he's struggling with a task, he asks for help—a much healthier approach than the one I usually adopt, which is to tell anyone who offers advice to go lie down in traffic. No wonder my game hasn't improved in 15 years.

6. Don't dwell. I have as easy a time forgetting a bad shot as I do a poor tax return. This inability to let go usually produces a downward spiral that derails the entire round before I hit the turn. Julian's attitude is the constructive opposite. If he's playing with a toy and one of its pieces falls off, he flips that toy aside and moves on to the next. If he really gets frustrated, he might have a brief meltdown—but three minutes later he's as happy as a spaniel and ready to tackle the thing again. Boy, that kid has a lot to teach me.

The Fakahatchee Whisperer

Soon after any sport captivates the masses, its participants seek a return to its original, purer state. No sport is immune to this syndrome. Today we lament the materials that allow tennis players to transform fuzzy yellow balls into rocket boosters, stripping away the game's grace and beauty. We become livid when a professional basketball player making ten million dollars a year demands an increase because one of his peers is making a few thousand more, making it appallingly clear to us that the game is no longer played simply out of love. We condemn symmetrical, retractable-roofed, VIP-boxed baseball domes as symbols of soulless corporate money-grubbing and celebrate those whose outfield walls feature an unusual angle or two.

Its popularity still snowballing, golf's participants have begun to devote plenty of lip service to the look and feel of the courses they play. The odd thing about this trend is that, while the average baseball fan could sound off for hours about the practical and spiritual differences between Astroturf and grass, most golfers, if asked to describe what separates a good course from a bad one, would have little to say.

But they'd know this: Part of today's collective longing for a purer golf state includes a deep appreciation for links-style courses. Though few residents of the western hemisphere actually know what a links course is, many are finding it fashionable to drop comments such as "That played like a links course" or "I understand they're going to build it links style," or perhaps "They should make this course more links style—you know, to make it more challenging."

It is generally accepted by the lay golfer that a links-style course is harder, though he doesn't actually know why. No matter. When any topic becomes trendy, those who enter into a discussion about it undertake a tacit contract to allow one another a handful of specific throwaway comments, never to be challenged. This allows us all to believe we are reasonably informed about the world when we in fact don't know much more than the names of the last few presidents and the lyrics to "Hotel California." As a result, when Martin Luther King Jr. comes up at a dinner party, anyone at the table is allowed to say, "I have a dream," and everyone else must simply sip their wine pondering the statement instead of asking for elaboration; and when someone declares, at any time, "Did you know our bodies are made mostly of water?", the person being addressed ought only to push up his bottom lip and consider the fact with fascination, whether or not he's already heard the statistic several dozen times before. This is why, when someone suggests that conversion to links style would increase the challenge a given course poses, those around him mostly just nod as though they were going to suggest the very same thing.

The truth is none of the people in the entire room have any idea what they're talking about.

Though I've never been to Scotland or played a true links course, standing on the first green at Eagles Nest in Richmond Hill, a northern suburb of Toronto, I feel more certain that I'm standing on a golf course in Scotland or Ireland than one in North America. Even a golfer who doesn't quite know what a links-style course is would probably know he were on one if surveying the same panorama I am now: a perfectly groomed, warmly inviting fairway lurking with mean rough, treacherous fescue and an inescapable allotment of pot bunkers. It is as though the course is an immaculately turned-out man in an Armani suit with a messy, unkempt shock of bleached hair.

I don't know how to design a golf course, nor have I any clue what goes into maintaining one. But, in the manner of all golfers whose ignorance about the finer details doesn't prevent them from evaluating a course, I tell Rob and Dave after only a single hole that Eagles Nest stands above virtually any public course I've ever played—and that I will make a decision before the end of the round whether it warrants my number-one ranking, in case anyone is wondering. Rob, having three-putted, ignores me. Dave, having landed in a bunker off the tee and taken an eight for the hole, is fighting the urge not to run into the highway adjacent to the hole.

Over the front nine, Eagles Nest gets us in the grip of its talons and doesn't let go. Rob sticks his approaches on almost every hole but putts as though he has the depth perception of a newborn. Dave somehow finds sand—either the deep, huge-lipped pot bunkers or the massive, amoeba-like waste bunkers—on each of the first six holes. On some holes he finds it more than once. I'm caught in the equally trying middle ground: decent consistency off the tee, neither spectacular nor terrible on the greens, but both compromised by a middle game more erratic than Courtney Love. Poor tee shots are one thing—okay, you say, so I messed up this hole, I'll just have to turn it around on the next—but frustration knows no depth like that produced by the sweet, center-stuck tee shot followed by the bungled approach.

However, these frustrations, and all the others produced by our unbalanced games, seem not to linger today as long as they usually do. The course has achieved something remarkable. It has transported three duffers to a place where the game matters less than the experience. The combination of pristine beauty and feral magnificence has hypnotized us. We find ourselves analyzing the layout of every hole but paying little attention to our actual scores, a transcendent experience.

Further legitimizing the links feel is the stunning view from the ninth tee: a gleaming lake and, beyond it, the clubhouse resembling a castle shipped from Scotland. My eight on the hole barely diminishes the pleasure I get from playing it. Nor does the eight I start with on the back half bother me much.

We drive our carts up to the par-4 twelfth tee to a vista whose sweep is almost surreal. From our elevated spot we can see no fewer than nine of Eagles Nest's holes, including multi-fingered waste bunkers, tiny fescued mountain ranges and impeccable fairways dotted by pot bunkers. On our fairway alone, we count seven pot bunkers and two waste bunkers. Normally this would unnerve us into silence and a good chance of soiling ourselves. Instead, we're effusive. Dave notices that each of the fairways is two-toned, the left halves a pretty light green, the right halves a deep forest green. I remark at the breadth of the view, astounded at how far we are seeing in each direction. Rob wonders aloud how long it will be before the course hosts a professional tournament. By the time we realize one of us is supposed to tee off, the course ranger has driven by and suggested it might be a good idea.

At the end of the round I card a 105 to Dave's 103 and Rob's 101. I've never enjoyed a 105 as much. I feel I've played a different kind of golf today. I almost feel as though I've played it in a different place.

Over the next several days, the wild beauty of Eagles Nest stays in my head. The experience of having played the course no longer satisfies me. I need to know more.

I call the course, introduce myself and ask if I might speak with the superintendent. "I'll transfer you to Brent Rogers, our Director of Turf Operations," says the receptionist. Director of Turf Operations? Perhaps I should change my golf title to Grand Master of Comedy Procedures.

I ask Brent if I might tag along with him one day while he performs his daily routine, which I assume involves turning on some sprinklers and perhaps edging a few fairway lines with a machine that resembles my neighbor's Weed Wacker.

Brent invites me to come by the following Saturday around 5:30, when he and his crew usually get things going. I'm surprised by the mention of a crew, though I suppose I should have assumed it would take a handful of people, not just one, to keep such a course looking as good as it does. I tell Brent I'll be there, though I wouldn't have thought daily greenskeeping practices begin in late afternoon. That's 5:30 a.m., he says. Oh, I reply, thinking maybe I can survive without knowing what goes on behind the scenes after all.

But my curiosity is too strong. The following Saturday, I steal out of bed in pre-sunrise darkness, hear Steph whisper, "Have fun with the turf guy," and, juice box and granola bar in hand, pull out of the driveway. Forty minutes later, glancing down at the directions Brent has provided—go a block west past the course, turn into the unmarked street on the left, then look for a building on the right—I arrive at what looks like a small warehouse just as dawn is beginning to break on the horizon.

As I park and turn off the ignition, I witness what looks like a small army mobilizing for battle. Out of a wide garage emerges a convoy of young men operating an assortment of vehicles that could be souped-up lawnmowers. All wearing the same navy windbreakers and resolute expressions, the young men strike out for the cart path.

I find Brent sitting on a golf cart and stroking the fur of his golden retriever, Keisha. Slightly gray at the temples, a small cleft in his chin, a glimmer in his eyes, he could be a better-looking Robin Williams. He extends his hand and welcomes me with the unmistakable enthusiasm of a man who wouldn't want any other job in the world.

The darkness continues to lift as he and I head out, as though God is gradually pushing up a dimmer switch. We pass an oval section of land the size of an outdoor swimming pool, which I assume to be a practice green and chipping area. I'm partly right, but it's for honing greenskeeping skills, not golf skills, Brent tells me.

"This is our nursery," he says. "I use it to let the guys experiment with different types of grasses, practise chemicals, fertilizers, get trained on how to cut a green properly, that kind of thing. It's also for donor turf."

"Donor turf?"

"If a piece of turf gets damaged on one of the holes—that could be approach turf, fairway turf, tee turf—and we need to replace it right away, this is where it comes from."

I never imagined a fairway needing an emergency turf transplant. Then again, when I consider some of the divots I've taken over the years, it becomes easier to believe.

"I did a rough calculation to estimate how many divots are created on the course in a week," he said. "The figure was over ten thousand. My team is responsible for filling those divots, and I want to make sure we do every single one properly."

Though I know nothing more about turf operations than calling Sheridan Nursery to ask when I'm supposed to fertilize my lawn, I can tell by Brent's expression of pride that this is a man in his element.

"It's like I have 18 different children out here," he says as we approach the first hole. "You get to know how to take care of them individually and also as a group, so they work in harmony. The one tucked away in the trees demands different care than the one out in the open, for instance."

Over the next two hours, I ride shotgun as Brent observes the efforts of the 25 or so worker bees in his charge. One of them is raking a waste bunker back and forth in careful parallel lines. Another is crouched over the fairway scrutinizing it like a child looking for grasshoppers. A third pushes a lawnmower in a perfect semi-circle around one of the greens, turning it magically from light green to dark.

Brent stops the cart to inspect the length of the freshly cut green against the older version of itself, informing me it should be just a hair above an eighth of an inch. Cutting greens this close is a relatively new phenomenon, he says. "The average golfer watches the game on television and comes to expect the same kind of conditions as he sees at the courses hosting major events, so people come to their local club and ask why it can't be like Shinnecock Hills. As the game becomes more popular, the expectations on us rise. We're now at the point where we have to ask ourselves how to achieve a certain level of speed on the greens without shaving them down to dirt. Every blade of turf grass is like a miniature solar panel," he says, running a fingertip over the new grass. "You shrink that panel down too much, and the plant can't subsist."

Today he's staying mostly in the cart to give me the verbal tour, but on normal days he'll walk every green, take soil probes and check moisture, all of which help him determine the level to set irrigation at for that evening. I ask him how different one day is from the next.

"I could walk out here at dawn and see one set of conditions, but by 11:00 a.m. it will be different," he replies. "A golf course is so dynamic. As any golfer knows, the course feels and looks different on the eighteenth tee than it did on the first. That's because everything's changing as the day goes on."

True. Usually my game is only slightly gruesome on the first tee but has changed to unspeakably hideous by the eighteenth. "I do notice that. So what are you looking for when you inspect the greens?"

"Abnormalities in color, density, dry spots, signs of disease. The trick isn't learning which diseases are which; it's learning how to anticipate them. Once you see it, it's often too late."

As we follow the twisting cart path, I gather a number of fascinating tidbits, among them the fact that the greens at Eagles Nest are 100 percent velvet, with velvet also constituting significant parts of the tees and the fescue. This comes as a particular surprise, since I could have sworn, based on my round, that fescue was part of the Venus flytrap family.

The tee areas really do look velvety, I tell Brent while admiring the light-green rectangular tee areas that look so soft, I have the mild urge to lie down and nap on them.

"Actually," says Brent, "they're about 90 percent fescue and 10 percent velvet. But because there are eight million seeds in a pound of velvet compared with only four hundred thousand in a pound of fescue"—he says this as though anyone with a third-grade education knows it—"there's really a greater density of velvet." I feel like I'm in high school trying to answer which weighs more, a pound of lead or a pound of feathers.

Brent apologizes for the blanched look of the fescue, explaining that, if it weren't for the unremitting heat of the past few months, it would have its usual golden wheat color and stand between 18 and 24 inches high. I feel like telling him the fescue looks just fine, but I'm still pretty angry with it for performing the disappearing trick on so many of my balls. But I do ask why, when it gets hotter, one can't just compensate with more water.

"The plant, physiologically, goes into a period of root decline once the heat starts," he says. "You need to supplement the moisture available in the soil. If you can't help the plant cope, its mechanisms start to shut down. It's a spiral dive. With the kind of heat we've had this summer, it's a constant struggle. At 7:00 a.m. it might look great, and by two in the afternoon it might be 90 percent dead. In those conditions, you can't get fancy; you just try to help it survive."

I peer at the course, imagining, as I've done before, grass as a living, breathing organism.

"And you can't just water indiscriminately. Timing is critical. If you water during the heat of day, you get wet wilt. The water heats up so much that, by watering the grass, you're actually scalding it."

"*That's* why they call it burning your grass," I say with an inadvertent hint of fascination. I clear my throat and look down as Brent eyes me like I'm Genghis Khan.

"Not to mention that the longer you have moisture on the leaf blade, the more you're creating an invitation for insects and disease."

"Well, I won't be watering the lawn at high noon again. Ha, ha."

"When I worked at a course in Vancouver," he says, "it was a special challenge, because the turf there is always wet and cool—the two key elements for disease to take hold. So we were always on our toes."

One senses that he loved then, as he loves now, the challenge—and the rush—of having to stay a step ahead of Mother Nature. I ask him if he grew up out west. "I grew up here, on a horse farm." The picture is starting to become clear. Caring for the land is in his blood. "I would caddy for my dad when I was maybe eight years old, so I became familiar with how a course looked and felt. When I was a teenager, we moved north, to the lake. I worked at golf courses for a few years and just kept staring out the window wanting to be outside. Eventually I worked at a course on Cape Breton Island, then the Vancouver stint, then some courses here, including Angus Glen, before landing at Eagles Nest."

Driving through the back nine, Brent stops to show me a hole that, due to the perimeter of trees around it, has its own microclimate. Humidity levels here, says Brent, are "just unbelievable. Down at the level of the turf, it's like a mini-rainforest. This was a tough summer. We had a lot of areas that were stressed. You can see here we suffered some disease patches." He bends to caress the damaged grass. "But we held on pretty good. The most important thing is to create a steady flow of oxygen. For example, you can see where we went in and cut some air lanes through that group of trees."

Air lanes. Now we're definitely not talking about my lawn.

"The ironic thing," he says, straightening, "is we have to abuse the turf a bit to take care of it. We cause it stress by cutting it every day, but we have no choice. Any time we can give that turf a break, I feel good. When it rains all day, preventing us from cutting it, I can practically hear it sigh in relief."

We stand together at the magnificent twelfth tee, whose perspective left me speechless a few days earlier and does the same now. I open my mouth to ask Brent how long the course took to build, but I don't get a word out. He's on a roll.

"See that large waste bunker in the middle of the three holes? Under there is a system that allows all our drainage to permeate the ground water."

I tell Brent I'm impressed by this information, though on the other hand I don't have a clue what he's talking about.

"The excess water gets directed back into the ground," he says. "Usually, runoff from a course is just discharged into a stream or other body of water. Seventy percent of our water is collected in underwater filtration galleries so that it's continually rehydrating the course. So we're not only growing grass, we're managing our use of the most important resource of all."

As we hop back in the cart and continue past a bunker at 13, I decide to stop asking questions. Brent is as chatty about the course as a parent whose child has just been called to the bar.

"Even though we have state-of-the-art irrigation systems, we do a lot of hand watering anyway. There are always abnormalities in the sand profiles. Did you know these sod-wall bunkers are built row by row? Yep—hand-built and hand-packed, top to bottom."

To the uninitiated, bunker construction would seem simple: cut hole in ground, pour in sand, repeat when necessary. I'm learning it's a little more sophisticated than that.

"The dozer will come in and shape it, then Doug will come out and paint the idea of the bunker he wants," says Brent, referring to the course's designer, Doug Carrick, and grinning as he imagines a process he's probably witnessed hundreds of times. "I'll then stake a series of six-inch-tall, flexible masonite boards around the perimeter, mimicking Doug's outline. After that, a mini-excavator will come in and clean up. We'll connect drainage through one of the main feeder lines out in the fairway, then, finally, add the sand. See this steep face? It's lined with a fabric underneath that prevents washouts, so it allows the water to pass through but keeps the sand in place."

I'll never look at a bunker the same way again.

"You've got places like Augusta National where they've got a kind of radiant floor heating, little polytubes about four inches apart running beneath the course that allow for controlling the temperature of the sand mix and the turf. If the soil is too hot, the turf won't grow; if the soil is too cold, it won't grow. You constantly have to force yourself to think outside the box."

I ask Brent how he decides what parts of the course to prioritize given the daily time squeeze.

"The order of importance is greens, tees, fairways, rough," he answers, saying the words like a mantra. I'm reminded of the scene in *A Few Good Men* where accused Private Downey tells Tom Cruise's character, Lieutenant Daniel Kaffee, that the code followed by his group is simple and uncompromising: unit, corps, God, country. (Kaffee can't believe his ears—though he still manages to take down Colonel Jessup an hour later by shouting in his face until he admits to having ordered the Code Red.)

"How different would it be managing a course down south?" I ask.

"Totally different ballgame," says Brent, flashing a thumbs-up to the crew member nearly finished mowing the apron on 15. "Take a course in Florida. They're dealing with warm-weather turf grass; we're dealing with cool-weather turf grass. But the basic techniques are the same. You top-dress, you verticut, you aerify." I nod, suggesting I have the slightest inkling what he's referring to.

With each hole we pass and each feature explained, I realize more clearly that, though the course architect may receive all the glory for creating the course's look, it is the superintendent who creates its feel.

Not only is the greenskeeper's stamp more evident on a given day, it also changes with the course over time. Indeed, when I ask Brent about his own creative biases, he talks about his evolving style the way a writer might talk about finding his own voice after going through the inevitable phase in which he merely imitates others. "In my early years," says Brent, "everything was about stripes—striped greens, striped surrounds, striped roughs. It was too busy. Lately, I've found golf courses have started to look that way, too, so I've gone a bit simpler."

"When you play other courses, do you find yourself analyzing them?"

"It's a problem. Part of having this job means I can't play a golf course and just enjoy it. Instead, I'm analyzing it from the moment I step on the first tee."

I know what he means: It's been years since I could read a book and just enjoy the damned thing. "Do you do any work on the course off-season?"

"We do some work on the trees and handle all the administration and paperwork, but that's it. Once the frost hits, we can't do anything to the playing surface," he tells me with more than a hint of sadness.

My tutorial finished, Brent and I arrive back at the clubhouse. The sky is now a bright blue. The last few crew members drive into the garage, park their vehicles side by side in a tidy line, then hop out, nodding in acknowledgment of one another's efforts.

As I step out of the cart, I notice a smattering of golfers honing their strokes on the putting green. "Those guys have no idea what's gone on in the past two hours," I say, mostly to myself.

"We know we don't get a lot of attention," says Brent. "But that's not why we do it. We do it because we love this game. You know, many of my guys do their duties here in the morning and then play the course in the afternoon. It's the best way for them to appreciate the fruits of their labors. There's plenty of science that you need for this job, but we all consider what we do art, too."

Before leaving I visit Brent's office, where Keisha is waiting patiently, her tongue wagging in the climbing heat. Lining Brent's shelf are a variety of books on course design, several of which he is proud to show off. What he doesn't know is I'm impressed most by *Turf Times*, the newsletter he self-publishes just for his own team. The current issue of *Turf Times* features a vehement piece by Brent himself on players who take too long to putt.

After stroking Keisha behind the ears for a minute, I exchange a handshake with Brent and thank him for the experience. From now on, whenever I step onto a freshly glistening golf course, I'll see all that's happened in the hours before.

Still, something seems off. While I was won over by Brent's passion, I suspect he's an anomaly. No one could enjoy being a director of turf operations that much. Most supers, I bet, are probably just glorified gardeners executing their mowing and watering by rote, waiting for the end of the daily routine so they can get home to catch the latest *Friends* rerun.

I decide to give Mark Reid a call. Two summers ago, while playing The Breakers Ocean Course in West Palm Beach, I encountered Mark, the head superintendent, during his daily rounds. I only remember three things about him: his joviality, his thick Melbourne accent and the hilarious way that accent produced the word *fakahatchee*. I know Mark is responsible not only for the Ocean Course adjacent to the hotel but also the famous course ten miles away, formerly Breakers West, and now, in deference to its eminent course architect, The Breakers Rees Jones Course.

Golf in South Florida isn't like golf in Canada. Golf in South Florida doesn't pause for winter. I suspect Brent's emotional attachment to his course results from having to wait several months every winter before getting to care for it again. I make a bet with myself that a man like Mark Reid, having to be on the job every day, every week, every month, is all business. He won't have time for sentiment.

I also have a feeling the throwback design and inherent unruliness of Eagles Nest makes it an emotional lightning rod for Brent, like a child you love even more because you're aware his nature is a little bit evil. Eagles Nest is young, wild and mean, like a Scotsman always ready for a scrap; The Breakers is old and immaculate, like a perfectly dressed lady of unmistakable pedigree, approachable and unthreatening on the surface but still able to make your life miserable.

I call and leave a message. Two days go by without a reply. Aha—I was right. He doesn't even care to talk about his job.

The third morning, Mark calls back. "How you goin', mate? Sorry it took me a few days—we're swamped here getting ready for the snowbirds." He means us northerners, massing to descend on all points south while our own golf courses our buried in hip-high snowdrifts.

I tell Mark I'd like to ask him about what he does for a living.

"Oh, sure, mate," he says. "It's in the blood. I'm the third in the family, mate. My dad's been a course superintendent for 40 years, my eldest brother for 20. I've been at it now for about 15. It's funny, mate, I always swore I'd never have any job like it, since it kept Dad away from home a lot. Then he came one day and jokingly said there was an apprenticeship at a nearby club called Barwon Heads. 'What do you reckon,' he said. 'Do you want to be an apprentice?' Mate, you know what I found out? I did."

"Um, okay, I guess that's a good place to start," I say, not actually having asked a question.

"Mate, I spent about four years doing that apprenticeship, then found out about a 12-month program offered by Ohio State specifically for young Aussies interested in the North American golf industry. I got a spot in that program at a course called Bear Lakes, and after about three months the superintendent offered me the position of assistant. That meant I could extend my visa for six months, mate. I ended up there more than two years."

"How does an Australian course compare to a North Amer—?"

"And here's the kicker, mate. While I was there I'd go straight from the course to the one pub where I could drink, since I was still young. There was a waitress there who always complained about us bad-smelling foreigners who didn't tip well. There's a reason I never went back to Australia. I married that waitress."

"Do you have ki—?"

"I moved on to Eastpointe Country Club in Jupiter, spent four and a half years there. I worked with a phenomenal super, chap by the name of George Kervern. Mate, that guy really knew how to grow grass."

Though he's only providing backstory, it seems like he's already in third gear. When I ask him about The Breakers, he really gets going.

"Mate, my job is ad-libbing. You can come in at 5:00 a.m. with one plan in your head, but the course will always throw something at you. I mean, you're dealing with Mother Nature, mate. You're dealing with a living entity."

He says this with a mixture of pride and reverence. If I mentally remove the accent, it could be Brent.

"When people clock out from their office job on Friday afternoon, mate, they know nothing's going to change between then and Monday morning. But a golf course is different. Mate, if a plant has a certain need and you wait a day to address it, that plant might be dead in the morning."

I ask him about the differences in caring for a golf course in Melbourne and one in Palm Beach. "Mate, everything's different, right down to the size of the raindrops—I'm serious, the ones here seem about four times bigger. It's a year-round industry here, mate. And Bermuda grass, as much as I've tried, can't be killed.

With bentgrass, you can get pithium, you can get stem weevils—those things will take you down before you even blink."

He continues, unstoppable, as though he and Brent have compared notes in advance of my call. He calls the holes on the course his babies, giving a passing nod to his three kids at home. He talks about watching the sprigs on a new course grow as though describing baby ducks hatching. He describes his two crews, together numbering about 50, as guys who look forward to rising pre-dawn every morning to make the course as attractive as it can be and then disappearing like leprechauns before a ball is struck. Like Brent, he describes his lawn at home as a picture of neglect. And, like Brent, he walks every green every day.

"Golf is played on the greens, mate," he says. "If you give them the right attention, they'll tell you what they need, whether it's top-dressing or verticutting or what have you."

Top-dressing and verticutting again? Don't these guys speak English?

We chat for about 20 minutes. Mark's enthusiasm for his job drips from every word. It's the kind of enthusiasm you can't fake. "Here's the bottom line, mate. I live to look after something that's also living. The best time of my day is when the sun comes up, and the second best is when the sun goes down, because there's nothing better than watching the sun rise or set on a golf course."

I thank him and hang up, smiling. Maybe this really is the best job in the world.

One for the Ages

The eighteenth at Silver Lakes is intimidating, not because of the hole itself but because I'm a bad golfer. This has served to make holes one through seventeen pretty tough, too.

Regardless, I'm in it. In fact, that's an understatement. As we come to the final tee, I'm up two strokes. It all comes down to this. One hole for all the marbles.

Because I haven't been overly consistent this season—apart from being as consistently inconsistent as usual, which I suppose counts as consistency—I was hardly overflowing with confidence going into the tournament. I haven't won one all year among our foursome, though I keep coming close. Dave's had the best year of any of us, usually carding scores that wouldn't make the local club pro sit up and take notice but might impress the guy who sits at the adjacent cubicle.

I haven't managed to break 100 yet, though I keep threatening it with frustrating regularity. Every golf course in the Greater

Toronto Area is by now aware it shouldn't be concerned if I start the round well, have a nice run around the turn or even manage a couple of pars. *Don't worry*, one of the other courses will remind the one I'm playing, *he'll put up a couple of 8's before it's over.* And inevitably I do record those abominable snowmen, blighting my card for eternity and leading to the same self-directed monologue all recreational golfers have after every round. *If I hadn't rushed that shot on six, I bet I'd have made par. That would have made me more relaxed for the tee shot on seven, which wouldn't have gone into the woods. Plus, my putting would have been better during the next few holes, and I think I three-putted at least twice over that stretch. I also should have left the driver in the car this morning. Stick with the 3-wood and I bet I'd have been nailing drives down the middle all day. There's five or six strokes right there. And that flub on 14. It's so simple; just keep the front arm stiff. Those shots shouldn't even count. I mean, I know what I should have done. So it's actually more like a 92 than a 108.*

It's the last week of September. Silver Lakes, like every other course, has transformed from vibrant greens to dazzling golds and russets. The air is still warm, still sweet, though underneath there is the tiniest hint of something crisper. A slight breeze wisps past my arms, letting me know the dog days have passed and the cycle is soon to shift again.

Approaching the eighteenth tee, the four of us chew the fat, each pretending we don't know the others' scores. Each of us, of course, knows exactly where he stands. I'm at 97. Dave is at 99, Rob 100 and Andrew, having one of those days, 106. (The prognosis for his round was made clear when he went bunker to bunker at the fourth three times before finally picking up his ball and saying, "Give me a ten and let's get the hell out of here.")

Rob, having made par on the previous hole, is up first. As he braces his legs as if trying to kill a team of ants under each foot, I mentally revisit the debate we've had for years about which of us owns the ugliest swing. This debate is a fascinating one because each swing is so unique in its offensiveness. All morph a bit over time, but the general nature of their horridness stays the same.

To me, Rob's, characterized by that sudden tensing of the legs, is the funniest because I always imagine that some stealthy figure has sneaked up behind him and yelled, "Hurry! Five Seconds! HIT!" I often wonder how he comes out of address, since his feet tend to appear as though they've been screwed into the ground during it.

He hauls off and sends one, as usual, left. The ball disappears past a thicket and settles somewhere in one of those mysterious patches one can't quite see from the tee. The ball could be part of history, or it could be sitting in lovely position for a second shot.

Dave, having bogeyed 17, is next. His stance this season has become progressively closed because of a tip given him by a golf pro in late March. With each drive that stays relatively straight, he closes off the stance a bit more, bringing him to the current version, his two feet so far from parallel it seems he has started to take a step forward before taking his shot.

His other amusing habit is to waggle his club a precise number of times before every shot while lifting and lowering his front foot. The number of waggles changes from year to year, but over the course of a season it's always the same. This season, it's five, no more, no less. The rest of us feel obliged to count out the waggles for him, usually making him stop, turn and give us a stern look, then begin the routine over again—at which point we restart the count.

In this case, his closed stance and five waggles combine to produce an outcome which immediately gets me anxious. His ball launches itself gracefully toward the fairway, begins its descent and plops down dead-center, an easy mid-iron from the green.

"Too bad," I say. "Can't do a thing with that."

He doesn't respond. In the heat of competition, Dave becomes mirthless, making him even funnier. When I say something like I just have, he doesn't smile. Instead he pauses, searching every possible scenario in his head to determine whether there is any way the shot he just mashed could actually have resulted in a bad lie, despite the fact that his ball is visible in the center of the fairway.

"I believe he's joking, kiddo," says Rob. "You can stop worrying."

"I wasn't worried," Dave responds. He's still eyeing his ball.

Andrew's primary issue is one of balance. His feet, philosophically opposed to the suggestion of standing over a golf ball, revolt with everything they're worth, causing him to look as though he's standing on hot coals while trying to settle into address. At the top of his backswing, his brain joins in the mutiny, triggering an imbalance that causes him to totter toward his back foot. The result is a strange noodle-like swing in which the club swishes lazily downward as though its mind is elsewhere.

I grin, tasting victory, as his ball soars nearly straight upward as though shot out of a cannon tilted too far toward vertical.

"Looking good for Skeeter," says Rob.

"Still time to mess up," murmurs Dave, with as much humor as Stalin on a good day.

I'm last up. My playing partners would be well justified in viewing my swing as the scariest of the lot. At some point between the ages of 14 and 20, I misplaced the second half of my backswing and haven't been able to find it since. The result is an abrupt, torque-heavy spanking motion whose only positive trait may be that it gets to the ball long before the ball expects it.

In a flash of intelligence I imagine must have overcome Einstein moments before he conceived the Special Theory of Relativity, I decide to replace my driver and hit a safe 4-iron instead. With a two-stroke cushion, it doesn't make sense to be reckless.

It's unfortunate that I forget I can't hit a 4-iron until half-way through my backswing. And since my backswing itself is only half the length of a normal one, I have even less time to address the thought than the average golfer. "Crap," I hear myself say as the 4-iron comes down and skulls my Top-Flite, probably making the Top-Flite wonder what it ever did to deserve this kind of treatment.

But the gods are smiling on me. While this drive won't end up on any highlight reels, it will forever belong to that most glorious of golf categories: bad shot, good result. The skulled ball, never reaching a height of more than ten feet, sizzles all the way out to the middle of the fairway, nearly the same distance as it would have through the air. Rob, Dave and Andrew look as though they want to bludgeon me. "Hey, when you're good, you're good," I say.

Our normal banter becomes intense silence as we approach our respective drives, each of us calculating every scoring permutation that will allow us, and not the others, to win. A small amount of money is at stake; more important is the degree of pride. Still clinging to my lead, I believe I know how Nicklaus and Palmer must have felt, how Woods and Singh must feel, striding toward their balls on the last hole of a major as the gallery applauds, breathless to discover how the drama will play out.

In fact, there are really only two differences between our tournaments and theirs. First, the only group in our vicinity that might count as a gallery is an assemblage of Canada geese that seem more preoccupied with honking at one another than the outcome of the match. Second, regardless of who comes out the winner today, his score will equate to nearly two rounds by Jack, Arnie or Tiger. Otherwise, this might as well be Augusta.

Andrew advances his initial pop-up 120 yards more, only now pulling even with Dave's initial shot. "So much for a late charge," he says. In our tournaments, only when one is out of it by six strokes in the middle of the final hole can he finally resign himself to self-deprecation.

I arrive to find my ball resting a pebble-toss short of the 150 stick. My angle to the green is clear, with only a small bunker to its front right posing a threat. The shot clearly calls for a 3- or 4-iron. I take out my 5-iron—not because I'm feeling strong, but because I have about as much confidence with a 3 or 4 as I would with a flugelhorn. My club selection on a given shot has less to do with the distance to the hole than with the fact that I hit only two clubs with fair consistency: my 5- and 8-irons. So I use my 5-iron for shots that require a 3-iron through 6-iron and my 8-iron for shots requiring a 7 through 9.

I step up, knowing that, even if I catch my 5-iron perfectly, I'm not going to make that green. But the macho part of my brain has engaged in a fierce battle with its rational side. *Pound this sucker*, the macho side is saying. *You can make this. Who cares if you've never hit your five that far before? Murder the thing. I bet you'll make it easy. You won't just win this tournament, you'll win it going away.* The rational side counters: *If we stay conservative and just hit it 160 like we know we can, then we'll have an easy chip to the green. Andrew's out of it, Rob isn't going to catch us, and it will put the pressure on Dave to hit a great approach.*

Easy chip? says the macho side. *There's no such thing as an easy chip. Anyway, chipping is for pussies. Hit the stuffing out of it and you won't have to worry about chipping.* I wait for the counterargument, but, to be fair, there really isn't one.

I stand over the ball waggling my 5-iron, my grip too tight, my breath too short, my expectations too high. My mental desperation manifests in an anguished swing that looks as if I am attempting to crack every rib in my body. The ball hooks hellaciously right, lands 160 yards away, then bounces once, twice, rolls past the edge of the sand trap, and comes to rest near the top of a hill sloping away from the green.

Dave, not displeased but wishing I'd done even worse, takes a 7-iron—his own comfort club—and waggles it five times, his front foot rising and falling with each waggle as though playing an invisible bass drum. He brings the club down, sending the ball toward the green on an upsettingly promising arc. Mentally I attempt to make the ball drop straight down out of the air or continue flying past the green, but apparently I still haven't learned telekinesis. Dave's ball skips stylishly past the flagstick and rolls to the apron. He's on in two.

We stroll ahead again, closer to the finish neither we nor the harried geese can predict. Part of golf's entrancing rhythm is that its greatest anticipation occurs not when a golfer is actually taking a shot but when he is marching from one to the next. We stroll forward together in silence, then fan out toward our balls.

I arrive at my spot trying to exude confidence, even though inside I'm freaking out. The average hacker, on at least half of his shots, has only the vaguest idea of what he is actually trying to accomplish. My ball is perhaps 30 yards from the hole, the only thing between us a bunker the size of a plastic kiddie pool. But the hole might as well be six miles away and the bunker a barracuda farm, because the longer I stand over this shot, the less I know what to do with it.

The pitching wedge in my grasp poses a major problem. For a recreational golfer, a good drive will travel 220, maybe 240, yards. Rarely does it fly straight, but, if caught properly, it will at least fly far. Between 200 yards and about 80 yards similar reliability exists via fairway woods, 3-irons, 4-irons and so on, up to the high irons.

Inside 80 yards, most of us weekend golfers become circus acts. No longer can we just say, "I hit my 6-iron one-fifty," take our normal swing and hope for the best. We are now in the dreaded shotmaking zone, which is like being asked to wrestle a grizzly and, for the most part, wing it.

The wedge wasn't part of my normal set; I don't remember when I bought it, and I can only surmise that it must have impressed me the way some people can give a great interview before showing their true incompetence once awarded the job. I can never visualize properly with it, and I suspect it's too short for me as well. Its shape is all wrong. Anytime I place it against the ground behind my ball, I have visions of bad things occurring. Most of the time, these visions come true.

I remind myself of the importance of not getting creative. I need only take a good, normal swing and trust that the club will do the job its designers intended. Often on shots like this

I straighten up too quickly, nubbing the ball off the toe. I issue another self-reminder, then a second, then a third, to stay down on the ball and keep my wrists firm. I can feel the stares of the others. Each of them is willing something different to go wrong with this shot. I resist their energies and remind myself one last time to stay down on the ball and just let the club do its work.

I take a three-quarter backswing, bring the club forward, straighten up too early and send the ball off the toe. As I shake my head, trying to untangle the cruelty of life and also deciding which method to use to kill myself, the ball scoots left, skirting the edge of the green, then comes to rest in the second-cut rough. I stand there awhile, still shaking my head, conspired against by every organism and force in the universe. I stare at my ball, perplexed as to how this could have happened. I don't understand anything. I feel my brain melting.

Rob's drive, which indeed ended up a souvenir for the trees, has left him a penalty stroke behind on the hole and effectively out of the running, unless both Dave and I collapse. Largely due to his anger over the penalty stroke, Rob has drilled his ball over the green and down a hill on the opposite side, where he now stands in an attempt to loft a shot back up and on. Seething, he gets into address, takes a weak swing, and pops the ball up 14 feet, where it lands just short of the crest and rolls back half the distance to where he's standing. "Are you serious?" he says. "Are you SERIOUS?"

"Looks pretty serious," says Andrew, who, with three more shots, has finally zigzagged his way onto the green.

Without a moment of preparation, Rob taps his next shot safely to within ten feet of the pin, demonstrating the irony of amateur golfers: Analyze the shot, and you're bound to blow it. Walk up and hit the thing, and you'll probably put it in the hole, or at least close.

Andrew two-putts from six feet, taking seven on the hole and finishing at 113 for the day. He tips his invisible hat to the geese, then tosses his ball up and, with a solid baseball swing, sends it into eternity. "That's better," he says.

Dave and Rob stare at me as I stand over my ball, picturing the shot. I decide it looks like a pitch-and-run. The fact that I don't know how to hit a pitch-and-run is a fundamental problem. I think I read once that you're supposed to lead with your front arm. Or is that back arm? No, that's to keep the ball low. Wait, that's placing the ball back in the stance. Son of a bitch, I have no idea what I'm doing again. I'm thinking of offering each of the guys ten bucks to let me put the ball back at 120 yards and just hope to knock it in with my 8-iron.

"I just thought I'd mention I have a meeting next Tuesday," Rob says. Dave is silent.

"Okay, okay," I say. "Just deciding on a club." I'm holding my 7-iron and, of course, my eight. I toss the seven aside, clear my throat, adjust my sleeve and get into address. I look up at the hole, visualizing. *Okay, relax. Scoop it just over the cut—well, don't scoop it; swing down on it; down; down; down—then land it about eight feet in and let it roll the rest of the way. Imagine if it went in? Their jaws would drop. What a way to finish.*

I clarify the situation in my head. Dave lies two, I lie three. His putt is tough, but makeable. That means I have to get this within one putt to at least ensure a tie.

"When did you say that meeting was?" Andrew says.

"Okay, okay."

I lift the 8-iron into my half-backswing and, as I start to come through, find myself trying to remember whether I applied sunscreen before the round. This break in concentration is sufficient to loosen my wrists just enough to turn my intended pitch-and-run into a sluggish tap, as though the club head has stumbled drunkenly into the unsuspecting ball—and shoved it ahead three feet.

Still away, I'm lying four. Dave is trying to suppress a grin.

"Quite the chipping clinic," says Andrew. I hope he walks into a puddle.

"I guess I'll cancel that meeting," Rob adds. I hope he walks into a tree.

I'm now on the first cut of green, maybe 18 feet from the hole. Dave has suddenly made up the two shots on me, which makes me want to scratch my eyes out. I try to calm myself. No big deal—it's just a putting competition now, and everyone knows I'm one of the four best putters among us.

Facing a long putt, Nicklaus says you should aim to get it within a club length of the hole. I'd be happy to get this within a block. I take my ritual two warm-up strokes. They feel right. The image of the ball dropping over the lip and into the hole is as clear to me as the pair of hot dogs I'll be consuming after the round. I shuffle my feet a little closer to the ball, look up, breathe in, pause, breathe out, look up again, calculate, calculate, calculate, feel the weight, imagine it, lock in the vision, see it, feel it, breathe in, see the putt, feel the putt, calculate, breathe out, and ... whack it harder than I meant to. The ball jumps off my putter and whizzes toward the hole. Dave can't suppress the grin this time as my ball passes through his legs and keeps rolling. He, Rob and Andrew watch it continue to the opposite edge of the green, 12 feet from the hole. I look at my putter, astonished.

"That was not how I saw that happening," I say, drawing laughs from Rob and Andrew and tempting the corners of Dave's mouth upward.

"Looking good for Dave," Rob says.

I'm still away. I cross the green to my ball, nodding at Dave on the way. Exhaling as much fury out of my body as possible, I stand over my ball, look once toward the hole, and swing. The ball skates along, searching for the hole to the right at first, then veering left. It continues to veer, like a sprinter coming around a turn. All four of us have the same thought: That thing's going right at the hole.

It keeps rolling, leaning left as much as it can, but doesn't quite find the side door. Instead it stops, agonizingly, an inch from the edge. I tap in for seven, wondering how in the name of Jean Van de Velde I just gave away five strokes. Dave now needs only to two-putt to win. I try to convince myself I'm dreaming. My brain issues a blameless response: *Sorry, but we're bad at golf.*

Rob takes a moment to consider his ten-foot putt, raps it about six feet, says "Have some balls, you idiot," then sinks the remaining four-footer to card, like Andrew and me, seven, giving him 107 overall. He takes three range balls from his bag, places them in a neat little row along the ground, and clobbers them into the trees.

Dave crouches behind his ball. He's about eight feet from the hole. My only hope rests in the fact that his path, after about two feet of plateau, becomes slightly downhill, and being asked to putt downhill, to a weekend golfer, is like being asked to impart backspin from the top of a glacier.

Dave walks to the other side of the hole, crouches again and holds his putter up in front of his eyes. He and I both know the likelihood of his sinking this putt is no higher or lower whether he considers it from the front of the hole or behind, left or right, standing on the green or manning a high-resolution satellite—but he's seen the pros use this technique and likes the way it feels.

"Should we call in forensics?" I ask.

"Hm," Dave responds, returning to his ball and getting into address. His club head is misaligned about two inches left of the hole, but I don't say anything. Andrew is relieving himself in the bushes, and Rob is practising his baseball swing with his 5-wood. Dave takes a last look at the hole, brings his putter back and taps at his Callaway as tentatively as if it contained a nuclear warhead. The ball rolls a foot and a half before coming to rest.

All eyes are on Dave. The mental resilience of any golfer can be measured in the instant he stands up after missing an easy putt. It is in this moment that he must use every fiber of his being to prevent himself from doing what he so desperately wishes to do: roar expletives that would be forbidden at a brothel, plunge the putter head into the softest part of the green and twist it around as though the green were the course's heart and the putter his sword, heave his bag into the nearest lake, tear out several clumps of his hair while spinning in circles like a ballerina set on fire, then sprint away in an indeterminate direction toward an unknown destination. Instead, being an adult assumed to possess composure and reason, he must stand up slowly, perhaps let out a sigh, look briefly confused, then, at worst, flick aside a piece of dirt with the putter head and tap the green three or four times.

Dave exhibits impressive poise, straightening almost as soon as the ball leaves his club. "Interesting," he says. After playing with him for two decades, I know that when he says "Interesting," what he means is, "I don't deserve to live."

"Tough one," I say. After playing with me for two decades, Dave knows that when I say "Tough one," what I mean is, "I'm thrilled you just did that. I never want to forget this feeling. I'm still dying inside from what happened to me just a minute ago, but I'm ecstatic nonetheless."

Suddenly, everything's changed. Dave has to sink a downhill six-footer just to tie me. Seconds ago I wanted to destroy the universe; now I want to kiss everyone in it. As Dave lines up his putt, his aura severely darkened, I think about how much despair one is willing to bear on a golf course just for the few moments of happiness it offers. Off the course I'm a levelheaded, relatively calm person. On it, I might as well be Mr. Hyde.

Dave lines up the six-footer for what seems like hours. I look at my shoelaces, at the rear view of the hole, at the horizon. Rob and Andrew make predictions about whether he'll sink it or miss.

Finally, Dave settles over the ball. "Don't leave it short," I think I hear him murmur. He pauses, takes one last look, then starts the putter back.

The moment he makes contact, he straightens up and, his voice suddenly resembling that of a five-year-old, says, "Come ON!"

I search for an expression and fail to find a suitable one. Dave, scared to hit the ball past the hole, has tapped it less than a foot. I've just won the tournament, though, as is always the case, through survival rather than heroics. In our matches, the person who emerges victorious does so not because he takes his game to another level but because his game falls apart slightly less than those of the other three.

We exchange handshakes and smiles. In a week, we won't remember who won or by how much. What we'll remember instead are the sunshine and the conversation and the laughs. In the middle of a meeting we'll smile at a particularly well-timed zinger, though we'll have a hard time remembering the shot that preceded it. We'll remember how good it felt to spend a day walking among grass and water and sand and the pleasurable fatigue that resulted from our preposterous attempts at golf mastery.

A golf round late in the season always carries with it a certain level of wistfulness, since one has no way of knowing whether it will be his last before the following spring. Though today I have hit dozens of poor shots and only a handful of good ones, already I am anxious to play again. I keep playing, will always play, will play until I can no longer lift my arms, because the next decent shot, containing infinite promise and unthinkable joy, is always only one shot away.

The Scottie Principles

Amid the pleasant commotion of Don Valley Golf Course, I'm showing my golf swing to Scott Myles. Though exposing my swing to a golf professional feels a bit like showing an enormous beer belly to a modeling agent, I'm resolved to improve. My game, having regressed astonishingly over the years—a result of bad habits being allowed to establish themselves without ever being questioned—has become truly appalling. Worse, I can no longer depend on accidentally making the handful of good shots that, for most recreational golfers, allow the 95 other shots to be forgotten. These days, I might go an entire round without cracking one of those accidental beauties, left instead with 110 moments of misery to take home.

So I've committed to, at the very least, an experiment: I will take three separate lessons and, after each one, play 18 holes. I don't expect my scores to be sparkling, or even any lower, when the experiment concludes, since the attempt to replace inveterate bad habits with positive new ones can be more destructive than simply continuing along the same ugly path. I will merely seek some shred of evidence that there is hope.

Halfway through my third swing, Scott says, with a smile, "Okay, I.J. You're a baseball player, is that right?"

He's got me. Between the ages of six and ten, like so many other young boys, I played soccer in my community league, running up and down the field chasing a ball with my friends, savoring the quartered oranges at halftime, giving my parents endless opportunities for the family album. Then, one day during the summer of my tenth year, a friend forced me to accompany him to a tryout for a baseball team. After throwing the ball once and catching it once—the sound of the ball snapping into the leather of my glove was the most exciting sound I'd ever heard—I was claimed.

Over the next decade and a half, I played golf occasionally with my friends while my heart and intellect remained faithful to baseball. I would swing a bat while preparing spaghetti in my apartment; while listening to Billy Joel or Wynton Marsalis or the soundtrack to *Les Misérables*; while standing on a subway platform. Once, on a beach in Italy, I noticed a piece of driftwood that resembled, closely enough, the shape of a baseball bat. I snatched it out of the sand and, for the next hour, tossed pebbles in the air and tried to hit them off the bridge a short distance away.

As I entered adulthood—and, in time, fell in love, acquired material things and produced children—something else happened. Golf made its way into me. Suddenly, I found myself wanting to play as often as I could at as many different courses as I could find. I wanted to write about the game, about its beauty and subtlety. I found myself defending it to others who argued it wasn't a true sport.

I never foresaw the problem, nor could I have known how deeply it had settled. My eyes, my mind and my pen had embraced golf and were ready to immerse themselves—but that most powerful, most silent, most stubborn form of knowledge, my muscle memory, would not be so easily convinced. I would stand over a golf ball, start the club back, and the white, dimpled ball at my feet would become a red-stitched horsehide. I'd see a fastball coming toward me, headed for the inside half of the strike zone. In my head an automatic, irrefutable reflex would snap to attention—*That pitch is not getting by me*—and my hands would whip forward through the hitting zone, my mind already picturing a headfirst dive into third base. The result, almost invariably, would be a slice, a push or, if I lifted my head early enough, a ridiculous cross-body shank off the heel.

Scott and I agree on a joint mission to eradicate, one drill at a time, the baseball instinct from my golf stroke. Ever cheerful, improbably confident, Scott tells me we're going to do some great work together. Though suspicious that he may not understand what kind of student he's dealing with—I feel like he's a trapeze artist who has told an apprentice they're going to do great work together, not knowing the apprentice has an acute fear of heights—I nod.

Over the course of a half-hour, Scott gives me three principles to work on. First, positioning the toe of my club face properly on the backswing. My swing plane, he says, is too flat and my arms tucked too far in—the baseball swing taking over. He has me raise the club less than halfway into my backswing, then turn and observe the position of the toe, which ought to face straight up, not behind me.

"Now this is going to feel pretty weird for a while," says Scott, reading my mind, "but we'll get there. We're going to have to convince your muscles to change something they've become used to." He seems so confident, I can't help but agree.

We proceed to turning my wrists over at impact. This particular movement—that is, the absence of it—has become a hindrance equal to my swing plane over the years. I don't turn my wrists at all, at least not until it has ceased to matter. Instead I slide my hands through the impact zone, bringing the club face down onto the ball at such a poor angle that I have less chance of hitting it straight than I do of winning the luge competition at the next Olympics.

Finally, he has me work on letting the clubhead come down naturally, allowing the motion of gravity to dominate—as opposed to the usual motion of my hands yanking the club forward as though reacting to a firecracker. This proves the hardest issue to correct. I have an easy enough time pointing the toe up on the backswing, and rolling my wrists only makes sense, but my hands, I can see, aren't going to give up the baseball swing without a fight. Scott watches as, several times, I take a slow, easy backswing, toe pointed properly upward, then, almost involuntarily, jerk the club forward. Over and over I stab at the ball, unable to control the instinct even though I've reminded myself to do so less than three seconds earlier.

Eventually Scott gets through to me by simply jumping up and down. He can see I'm unable to accept the trampoline effect that allows a golf ball to ricochet off the ground and into the air. But when Scott bends his knees and jumps up, I understand. To go up, you must first go down—as must the ball. I'm resolved no longer to pick it clean, with only the strength of my arms pushing the ball into the air. I will pound this thing into the ground so hard it's going to look like a pancake in stop-motion.

When the lesson is done, Scott tells me we'll stick with just the three thoughts for today. Since he's been more patient with me than an obedience school instructor teaching a Rottweiler to mellow, I don't bother telling him my usual capacity for thoughts is one.

Preparing to tackle the course, my first thought is whether the rope at 18 still exists. I haven't played Don Valley in years, but I fondly remember a T-bar-like mechanized yellow cable that used to be in place to assist golfers up the steep rise between the eighteenth green and the clubhouse at the end of a round. My musing is interrupted when I spot my playing partner for the day, who represents the Scottie Principles better than anyone. Built like a Sherman tank, my friend Ira is the strongest, most talented athlete I know. But, just like a guy who weighs one-forty, to do well on a golf course he merely has to relax and let the swing flow.

It isn't easy to accept the concept that, by swinging lightly, one better summons his strength to the task of hitting a golf ball. *Don't I have to swing hard?* you hear your brain quite logically asking—but the day any golfer convinces himself of this truth is the day his game transforms.

As if to reinforce the message I'm trying to burn into my brain, we're placed with a beefy guy named Newton whose arms look like twin reticulated pythons. Amusingly, his voice is as high as his chest is thick, but I still get the message.

On the first hole, with my driver, I try to force myself not to aim right as I usually would. I remind myself of the Scottie Principles: toe straight on the backswing, just let the head drop on the ball, turn the wrists over through impact.

Remarkably, this works. The ball doesn't travel far, but it travels straight. I want to buy dinner for anyone within a ten-mile radius. Application of the Scottie Principles works similarly over the next several holes with my 3-wood and 5-wood. I try to keep my excitement contained, but it's bubbling.

On the par-3, 177-yard fifth, I pull the 4-iron out of my bag, even though every cell in my brain is telling me to float a 3-wood. No, I say to myself. Take the 4-iron, apply the principles and just try. I do. The ball jumps off my club, sails toward the green and lands pin high. Ira asks me a question but I don't hear it because I think I might be having an orgasm.

I battle my instincts even harder on the par-5 sixth, a dog-leg left, tailor-made for my slice. I stay faithful to the principles, and, amazingly, the ball again ends up straight. On the same hole, Newton hits a thunderous ball off the tee. His game is frequently spectacular but, in the end, as mediocre as ours.

The spectacular moments, however, are truly spectacular. On the 295-yard eleventh, Newton pulverizes his ball all the way to the green. As he settles into address to attempt his 15-foot eagle putt, I wonder to myself why, when another player is standing over a putt, it always seems like he's going to make it, but when one is standing over a putt of his own from the same distance, it seems the odds of making it are one in several trillion. Newton disrupts my thought by rolling his ball over the front lip and into the hole. As it rattles into the cup, Ira and I let out a collective whoop and sprint toward Newton to exchange high fives.

While Don Valley may be relatively short, its natural topography helps make it deceptively challenging. The par-4, 375-yard fourteenth is a prime example. Ira, Newton and I all hit what feel like solid drives toward a rising dogleg. But each of our balls hits the middle of the doglegging hill and bounces back to its base. Newton, irresistibly tempted by the thought of hitting over the trees on the left, grants himself a mulligan. Though he crushes his ball as usual, it fades into the trees about two-thirds of the way up.

Our blind second shots up the hill and around the dogleg produce no better results, putting us at equal risk of not reaching the green within three. Like many of the holes at Don Valley, what seemed like an easy par from the tee has become sinking hope for a bogey.

We get our bogeys, aggravated. But our collective annoyance is eased by observation of the groups behind and ahead of us. At our backs are four elderly ladies who hit the ball so short but so straight that not once, but twice, their balls end up forming a perfectly straight line in the fairway separated equidistantly by 20 yards or so, like one side of a landing strip. In front of us, four teenage boys, their shorts and golf shirts hanging loose on their bony frames, are spraying the ball all over the course from tee to green, but their laughter and enjoyment take the edge off the frustration of waiting for them to advance.

Then there's the fact that my 3-wood has stayed relatively straight all day. I feel I'm still swinging off my back foot, but, while the gravity principle and the turning of the wrists continue to be incredible psychological hurdles, they have more than proven their validity. Scottie Myles is a genius.

But every subject needs time to master the lesson. On 18, I show my true stripes. After fading my drive into a sparse cluster of trees, I try to punch out into the fairway with my 5-iron, but hit it too high. My ball finds the lowest-hanging branch of the tree 15 feet in front of me and ricochets back, ending up 15 feet to my left.

"What are the odds you can hit the same branch?" Ira shouts. I take another swing with the 5-iron and, somehow, nail the same branch. The ball rebounds again, this time ending up on my right. I finally manage to reach the green two strokes later and ultimately scrawl a lamentable seven in the final box on my scorecard.

I'd wished only to see improvement in my swing, if not in my score. Both expectations have been met. My swing feels something like a golf swing, which I've not been able to say since I picked up a club as a teenager and started whacking away, thinking little about the mechanics of how to do it. But since most strokes in golf are taken from inside 100 yards, and since I'm still horrendous from this distance, I card 104 despite the apparent improvement. And I find I don't care. As Newton, Ira and I grasp the yellow pulley and haul ourselves up the hill between 18 and the clubhouse, I feel something I haven't felt on a golf course for a long time: promise.

The next afternoon, Don Valley buzzing anew, Scottie is asking me to pose. Relaxing the swing, he says, is only part of the solution; just as important is bringing it all the way through to finish. My inside-out baseball swing tends to wind up in a kind of awkward coil around my ribcage. Scottie says he wants me to bring the club up and all the way through until I can tap the toes of my back foot against the ground and not stumble backward.

At first I don't understand the point. Then I take a swing, hold the finish, and, at Scottie's request, lift my back foot to tap the ground. I stagger backwards. It's a moment of epiphany, and I can see from Scottie's grin that he knows I understand. It's not just about rhythm; it's about balance.

We continue to practise this simple yet profound adjustment for most of the half-hour. I feel transformation. I sense that

Scottie is pleased by my enthusiasm. To him, I must be like a child just realizing his own potential where he'd convinced himself there was none; a child willing to learn; a child who is *coachable*.

Though nervous to apply two lessons' worth of principles at the same time, I can't wait to hit the course. My lesson ended at 4:00; our tee time is 4:16, when most groups will be heading back to the clubhouse having just completed their rounds. We'll be fighting the sunset a few hours from now.

My brother-in-law Richard appears outside the pro shop doors just as I'm telling Scottie to have a good day. Richard asks me how the lessons are going. I don't want to let my excitement turn into foolish hype, so I tell him they're not going badly. I want to tell him I'm pretty sure I can get my tour card within six months.

After one shot, I'm glad I didn't hype my improvement. Trying to integrate everything Scottie has taught me and therefore executing none of it, I lose the ball into the woods, then hit a branch off my drop, then sail a ball over the green. While this pattern of shots is customary, something has changed. Despite the seven I'm likely to pick up to begin this round, I feel okay with myself. True, I hit into the trees with my first shot, but it faded more than it sliced. For me, this is an accomplishment equivalent to piloting a hot-air balloon around the world.

Richard is an ideal playing partner for two reasons. First, though a deep, complex human at the core, he's really made up of only two traits: optimism and compassion. No matter how you're performing during a given round, he'll manage to both convince you it's going to get better and sympathize with your desire to commit hara-kiri on the spot.

Second, his stance is hilarious. Because he's a large guy, irons in particular look twig-like in his grasp. Adding to the humor, he holds the club extremely low, as though he's about to place it on the ground and walk away, before swinging. When he does swing, he keeps his head down as the ball flies away—usually pretty far, and often pretty far left, since he has a hook as chronic as my slice.

My combination of anticipation and nervousness produces an ugly seven-eight to open.

"You'll find your game," Richard says. That, of course, isn't what I want. I want to lose my game and find a different one.

On the third, something remarkable happens to make me believe this might actually be possible. I bring my driver back, Scottie-fashion, come through the ball thinking about my finish, follow all the way through the swing and witness the ball traveling straight toward the fairway. The ball ends up six inches from the bottom of a three-foot-wide tree trunk, giving me an impossible lie for my second shot. But it went straight. I'm bursting.

Over the course of the round, this starts happening more. I still have my fair share of shanks, I still don't hit very long and I still have less finesse inside 100 yards than that displayed by a wrecking ball operator—but the good shots are starting to happen by design instead of occasional divine clemency.

"Your swing is looking much better," says Richard. "More fluid."

Hearing someone use the word fluid to describe any part of my swing makes me want to weep. But this isn't about transitory improvement; it's about lasting change. I remind myself not to get cocky.

The green clear, I push my tee into the ground and place the ball atop it. I issue myself one last reminder to concentrate on rhythm and balance instead of torque and speed. The ball flies toward the green and drops near the hole. I'm stunned and elated. My birdie attempt stops four feet short as I let my wrists go slack, but I sink the second putt and proudly record a thick, dark three on my scorecard.

Walking toward 16, I cast a glance toward the sun, which is sinking quickly.

"Gorgeous," says Richard, referring to the pink hues streaked across the thin cloudline. We play 17 in dimness, and 18 in the gloom, our last putts tracking toward the hole not as gleaming white balls but small shadowy ghouls. As the last light dies, we head toward the yellow rope creaking along its winch.

I see Richard off, then, using my headlights to see, tally my scores. My total is 106, two strokes worse than yesterday. Still, there's a difference in this 106 and every other 106 I've ever recorded. In the swings that produced this 106, there's potential.

I arrive the next day for the last of my three lessons. Scottie is chipper as usual, anxious to get me back on the practice tee. I suppose he sees me as the ultimate litmus test of his teaching skills. If he can turn my swing into something attractive, he should be able to bend thick steel bars by staring at them.

He asks me to hit a few balls with my 7-iron. I'm nervous to demonstrate the Scottie Principles to Scottie, but I close my eyes, try to relax and go through the messages. Close the face. Roll the wrists. Follow through. Tap the toes.

Click!

It flies straight. Scott smiles. I don't know if he's more pleased with himself or with me, and I don't care. I'm still admiring what I feel is the nicest 7-iron ever struck in the history of golf.

"Alright—today we're going to have some fun," says Scottie. "We're going to add distance."

We work on two things over the half-hour. First, Scott has me adjust the position of my back shoulder. Accustomed as I've been to coming over the top of the ball (and from the wrong angle, and with the wrong swing plane), I unconsciously misalign my shoulders to my feet, causing all sorts of problems that I can tell Scott barely has time to imply. Instead he takes the butt end of his club and pokes my left shoulder until it's farther back and lower down.

"That certainly feels awkward," I say, giving Scott a chance to admit he doesn't know why he just did that.

"Take your swing," he says. I do—and the ball flies 20 yards past the flag at which I was aiming. Scott tells me we're bringing my bigger muscles into play—those of my chest and torso, which until now have been forced to defer to my arms and wrists as a result of bad setup. I apologize to my chest, then ask Scott what's next.

He hands me my driver. "Let's go to the big wood."

I set up. He pokes my shoulder back. I bring the club down, think of my finish and smack it.

For several minutes I alternate between the 7-iron and driver, getting into address, having my shoulder adjusted—as though I'm constantly dislocating it and he's continually popping it back in—and hitting balls, for the most part, longer than I normally hit them.

"Take your glove off," says Scott. By now I know him well enough to recognize that this kind of statement signifies we're moving on.

He points to the worn part of my glove, near the bottom left corner of my palm.

"Because your glove is worn right here, you're losing distance." He likes to start me with riddles. Since I don't have a guess at the answer, I smile at him until he breaks.

"Most golfers, in a false attempt to gain distance, turn the handle too much into their palms."

Suddenly, I think I know the answer to the riddle. During the Christmas of my seventeenth year, I traveled with my rep junior baseball team to the poor Dominican town of Santo Domingo, a hotbed for eventual Major League shortstops, to play a series against a local team.

Before the first game, we were taken to a training camp run by the Blue Jays' head scout, Epy Guerrero. Standing amid the infield clay and white chalk lines, Epy had addressed us for fewer than ten minutes, but the single message he imparted hit me with the force of a landslide.

He'd chosen me to come up and asked me to squeeze his finger with my palm. Harder, he'd said. Harder. Come on, aren't you squeezing? My teammates chuckled. Then he laid his fingertip not across my palm but across my knuckles, and asked me to squeeze again. My palm had felt no more forceful than if I'd been watering the grass with a hose; but with my fingers, I felt the power of a vise grip. *Ow!* Epy had said, pulling his finger back. My teammates chuckled again, their eyes bright with understanding.

"Now," said Epy, "is it better to hold the bat in your palm or your fingers?"

Scott places the club handle in my palm as studiously as Epy had done with his finger. "This is how you have the club now," says Scott, before rotating the handle slightly so that it comes to rest more on the inside of my knuckles. "Now you see the heel of your palm, the fleshy part, pressing over the side. If you can re-move your bottom three fingers from the club, plus your thumb, and still swing it back and forth, you've got the right grip."

I attempt the seemingly simple exercise twice, three times, but my negative conditioning, perhaps sensing that it's finally being confronted, doesn't want to budge. Finally I accomplish it. My index finger is hooked around the bottom of the handle, the fleshy part of the heel of my palm providing support to keep it aloft.

"Okay, time to put it all together," he says. "Come on up."

I get into address thinking about my grip. Then I start thinking about my left shoulder. Then I jab at the ball and slice it into the trees. I turn to Scott with an expression like that of a six-year-old asking why his rabbit ran away.

"Don't panic," he says. "You probably found yourself thinking about a lot of stuff, trying to remember all the things we've talked about. What happens is your hands take over and speed up."

"The old swing," I say.

"The old swing. But don't worry, those swings are going to happen. Just slow down and try to trust the movement."

I get into address again.

"See that second flag?" says Scott. "I want you to aim for it."

After a short pause, I pull the trigger. The swing releases, the wrists roll and the ball soars toward the second flag, bouncing just short of it and scooting past. Scott is leaning on his club, smiling.

"All I did was get you focused on the target, so your mind was clear. You're working hard to burn the lessons in, and that's great. But think about all that stuff *before* you get into address, so once you're standing over the ball, you're ready to just fire away."

The last ten minutes of my lesson thus becomes a mental drill. Over and over, I stand behind the ball and think about my shoulder, my grip, my club face, my wrists and my toe-tap, then get into address and try to stop thinking about all of them.

Most of my shots travel fairly straight; most travel farther than usual. Still, among the promising shots are enough pushes, blocks and outright shanks to remind me that this is far from an overnight process.

"I.J., we've done some great work here," Scott says. "When you go out on that course today, I want you to remember you're still trying out new things. Don't worry about your score. Just practise good habits."

I proceed directly to the first tee, where I'm introduced to my playing partners for the round, Don and Ron. I try to remember that Don is the one with the mustache and Ron the one with a cigarette dangling from his lips. Then their friend Manny shows up, ruining the rhyming scheme. Manny's name proves even more troublesome over the course of the round, since every time I say something like, "Nice chip, man," or "That's a pretty drive, man," he probably thinks I'm presuming to give him a nickname.

Wanting to make Scott proud—and suspicious that he might be watching me via a series of hidden cameras planted throughout the course—I don't allow myself to address any ball without first visualizing the Scottie Principles. Most important is to remind myself to keep my hands from panicking. Don't jab at the ball, I tell myself before every shot. Don't jerk, don't stab, don't lunge. Eventually I refine it into the mantra *Don't jab, Don't stab*, which I immediately consider copyrighting.

The mantra does have a calming effect. Focusing more on rhythm and tempo than hitting the cover off the ball, I par the first, bogey the second. A mental lapse on the third causes double, but my swing, for the most part, remains slow and controlled rather than the apparent product of electroshock therapy.

Though my mind, insisting on slowness and control, is in constant conflict with my hands, who are convinced that pounding the hell out of the ball is the way to success, my game stays mostly quiet for most of the front nine. Don (I think) exhibits a model swing, textbook club selection and workmanlike effort on the greens. Ron (maybe), despite chain smoking the entire front half, displays a handful of neat shots among a pile of miserable ones.

It is the player with the least fundamental swing, Manny, who tempts me most toward the old ways. Manny's stroke, a ferocious downward chop combined with an extreme step backwards, might be the ugliest thing I've ever seen on a golf course, but it somehow produces decent scores. If he can succeed with that, I think to myself, why not just revert to what I was doing and play around the slice?

The *NO!* issued by my brain is as loud and startling as a thunderclap. As if to reinforce the point, Manny unravels heading into the turn, his fearsome chops suddenly propelling balls in every direction. Accompanying his erratic play is a stream of tight-fisted muttering that I sense doesn't fall into the category of self-affirmation.

On the 490-yard eleventh, the Scottie Principles come together to produce a handsome drive. I'm about to swing the 3-wood when a simple etymological revelation distracts me. *Just get it on the fairway*, I tell myself. Then, *Fairway! The fair way! Wow!* Yes, I realize, it certainly is the fair way to go—not fair as in just, but fair as in pleasant. According to the same logic, the rough should really be called the crapway.

My problem is keeping all the principles in my head at once. When I remember to close the club face, I forget to roll my wrists. When I remember to adjust my grip, I forget to follow through to toe-tap. Most people can easily memorize a phone number since short-term memory allows us to retain seven figures plus or minus two. I wonder to myself, after flubbing a 6-iron on 15, how many golf tips the average mind can retain.

When I do manage to retain two or three of the pointers at once, wonderful things happen. Swings stay rhythmic. Balls fly straight. Homicidal tendencies are kept to a minimum. Intriguing by-products also result, such as the consistent ball marks my approach shots keep causing on greens. I have no idea whether this indicates better golf, but having to use my ball repair tool so often makes me feel more impressive.

I walk toward the eighteenth tee knowing I've taken 93 swings. The hole is an easy par 4—easy, that is, if one suppresses the taste for adventure. To the small gulch protecting the green it's about 230 yards; over it, maybe 270. In other words, psychology, more than distance, determines one's score on this hole.

The fairway isn't overly narrow, but it curves far enough left that a wayward drive into the trees on either side leaves a player no choice but to punch out. The more devilish mental obstacle involves the lay-up to the gulch most players sensibly attempt. It all seems simple enough. Even a weak drive, as long as it finds the fairway, will require no more than a short iron to reach the green. But most golfers, lining up this second shot, forget the evil that imbues most course architects: The back contour of the green is lined by a short metal fence beyond which lies nothing but trees. Sail that fence and you've blown the hole. Good players hit their modest drives, walk up to their balls lying 30 or 40 yards short of the gulch, and think two things before they hit: First, get it over the gulch, and second, don't hit it too hard.

As so often happens in golf, the second thought obliterates the first. By the time the club comes down, the player is thinking not mostly, but entirely, about keeping the ball in play. The result is lots of wrists loosening at impact, plenty of heads lifting early and an incredible proportion of balls bounding or rolling straight into that gulch.

I tee off with my 3-wood hoping to fly the ball a safe distance into the fairway. I almost wish I weren't aware of the situation—for I know that, as long as I play this conservatively, I'm going to do the impossible. I'm going to accomplish the unheard-of. I'm going to break 100.

I swing slowly, easily, rhythmically, but push the ball none-theless. I'm still thrilled beyond words that it's a gradual fade rather than a physics-defying slice, but the fade is a fraction too severe. I'm in the trees.

Arriving at my ball, I indulge only briefly in the exercise of trying to convince myself I can thread the ball through the small opening in the trees, get a lucky bounce and land it on the green. I know from experience that the longer these ludicrous exercises are allowed to go, the more their ludicrousness starts to seem like creative shotmaking. I punch out.

I don't want to think too long about this shot. Ron and Don have let the hole get into their heads as well, Ron having blocked his drive far right, forcing a punch-out similar to mine, Don having gotten too much of his drive and rolled his ball into the gulch. Manny, hacking down on the ball and stepping backwards, has produced the only solid drive among us, setting himself up for an easy approach.

I'm about 90 yards to the green. Pulling my pitching wedge from the bag, I try to put the gulch, then the fence, out of my mind. I'm shooting for that flag, nothing else. I remind myself this is a full swing, not a chip. Then, just in case my muscles don't understand the directive, I clarify by indicating that I will have no choice but to kill myself should the ball end up in that gulch.

I swing, follow through and watch the ball seem to hover in midair as though freeze-framed. In reality it covers 30 yards, landing on the far bank of the gulch, rolling backwards and, finally, mercifully, infuriatingly, coming to rest against a small pile of twigs.

I cross the wooden bridge reminding myself I still lie only three. Get the ball up and on, two-putt and I've still done it. I place one foot awkwardly in a patch of dirt behind the twigs, the other on a plant beside them, and swing. The ball scoots onto the high grass between me and the green and, after about ten feet, stops.

Over the course of a golf hole, one is constantly adjusting his expectations, usually downward. At a certain point, those expectations turn from acceptable to galling. Two shots ago, I was thinking about saving bogey. One shot ago, double-bogey. In both cases I was equally untroubled, since both had me finishing under 100. Now, I'm just mad, since nothing less than a chip to within one-putt distance will save the hole and the miracle score.

At the same time, the pressure's off. The ball will get close enough to the hole or it won't, and I'll sink the putt or not. I'm still angry as hell, but maybe something strange and wonderful will happen.

Or maybe it won't. I bounce the ball onto the green, and it rolls—but not far enough. I'm 15 feet from the hole. I've taken 98 shots.

Though I don't assess my putt forever, it probably feels that way to Ron, Don and Manny. First I persuade myself it's left to right; then right to left; then straight. In the end I go with straight. I stand over the ball, breathe and bring the putter through. The ball begins tracking toward the hole. It's on line. It seems to have enough weight. My eyes become as big as quarters.

But it isn't meant to be, at least not today. The slope I failed to read starts pulling the ball left halfway to the hole. By the time it stops, it's missed by three feet. I drain the putt, landing squarely on the century mark.

I expect feelings of disappointment and frustration. But as I trade handshakes with Ron, Don and Manny, I find I feel quite the opposite: pleased, even uplifted.

At the car, changing my golf shoes for sandals, I realize why. In the past, my disappointment and frustration have resulted from there being no reason to believe my next outing would be any better. Now, that belief has shifted. I have the tools. I have the time. I have the commitment. I know there's a long way to go—down, at least on the scorecard. And that's all I need to believe, all any golfer needs to believe. Golf may be a game of constant aggravation, frequent second-guessing, even sporadic madness, but it is also a game of eternal, infinite promise.

About the Author

I.J. Schecter writes feature columns for top golf publications throughout the world, including *GOLF Canada*, *Golf Monthly* and *Fairways*, as well as a variety of other sports and fitness magazines. A National Magazine Award winner and author of a previous short story collection, *The Bottom of the Mug*, I.J. lives in Toronto with his wife, Stephanie, and his sons, Julian and Oliver, both of whom exhibit more golf potential than their dad despite being three and one years old.